Message Unsto[ppable]

Acts

CF4·K

We believe that the Bible is God's Word to mankind, and that it contains everything we need to know in order to be reconciled with God and live in a way that is pleasing to him. Therefore, we believe it is vital to teach children accurately from the Bible, being careful to teach each passage's true meaning in an appropriate way for children, rather than selecting a 'children's message' from a Biblical passage.

10 9 8 7 6 5 4 3 2 1

Copyright 2011 © TnT Ministries

34A Market House, Kingston-upon-Thames, Surrey, KT1 1JH

Tel: +44 (0) 20 8549 4967

E-mail: sales@tntministries.org.uk, www.tntministries.org.uk

Published in 2011 by Christian Focus Publications,

Geanies House, Fearn, Tain, Ross-shire, IV20 1TW

Tel: 01862 871 011 Fax: 01862 871 699

E-mail: info@christianfocus.com

Cover design by Tim Charnick

Cartoon Illustrations by Tim Charnick

Printed by Bell and Bain, Glasgow

ISBN 978-1-84550-616-2

Mixed Sources
Product group from well-managed forests and other controlled sources
www.fsc.org Cert no.TT-COC-002769
© 1996 Forest Stewardship Council
FSC

TnT Ministries (which stands for Teaching and Training Ministries) was launched in February 1993 by Christians from a broad variety of denominational backgrounds who are concerned that teaching the Bible to children be taken seriously. The leaders were in charge of a Sunday School of 50 teachers at St Helen's Bishopgate, an evangelical church in the City of London, for 13 years, during which time a range of Biblical teaching material has been developed. TnT Ministries also runs training days for Sunday School teachers.

Contents

Message Unstoppable: Acts

Message Unstoppable is a complete programme of six sessions designed for use at an after-school club. It can also be adapted for use in a variety of settings, such as holiday clubs, camps and church weekends away. The club is for 5-11 year olds, with separate teaching groups for infants (5-7s) and juniors (8-11s), and is suitable for both churched and unchurched children.

The club takes place in various immigration halls around the world. The children are on an amazing race around the globe moving from country to country. At each checkpoint they hear true stories of other "border breakers" from first century Palestine who took a very important message about Jesus from Jerusalem to people all over the world. By the end of the series the children should understand the good news about Jesus's death and resurrection and how that message spread despite some very radical opposition. They should understand their need for repentance and faith as well as their need to share this good news with those in their local communities and further afield.

The Bible teaching takes place in small groups and there are separate fun sheets for 5-7s and 8-11s. A fun packed programme includes games, creative craft activities, singing and puppets and there is also time for a snack. All the activities are designed to reinforce the teaching points for the day. Leaders accompany their groups through all the activities, giving plenty of opportunity to build relationships with the children.

Preparation of Bible material:
Thalia Blundell
Trevor Blundell
Sam Osborne

Editing:
David Jackman

Other Activities:
Kim Bell
Rory Bell
Trevor Blundell
Thalia Blundell

The Team

Your team is your most important resource and you need to plan and pray as a group. You should have regular team meetings to provide training and build up team spirit. These meetings should include the following:

- a review of the Bible teaching programme
- how to explain the gospel
- guidelines on working with children
- your safety policy and emergency procedures
- being good role models
- getting to know the children, learning their names and using them
- encouraging quiet children
- maintaining discipline from the floor
- being involved
- time to pray together

You need the following team members:

- *Minister of Foreign Affairs* (co-ordinator), who is in overall charge, leading up front, organising the warm ups, consolidation games and wind ups, and keeping the programme to time.

- *Immigration Officers* (small group leaders), who accompany their group throughout the programme and are responsible for the start up activity, Bible teaching and craft work.

- *Security*, who directs children to the appropriate registration or enquiry desk. He/she is also responsible for site safety and checking that children are met by an adult at the end.

- *Visa Application Personnel*, who are responsible for registering all the children and maintaining the master register. They can double up as the *Customs Officers.*

- *Customs Officers*, who are responsible for purchasing, serving and clearing away refreshments.

The following jobs need to be allocated:

- Musicians.

- Memory verse teachers, who decide how to teach the Bible verse and at which point in the programme. (Some fun sheets for the 8-11s contain puzzles to find the memory verse, so in those sessions it would be better to teach the verse after the Bible time.)

- Puppeteers or actors.

- Quiz Leaders.

- Technicians, who are responsible for setting up the OHP and screen, and any lighting or sound system that is required.

- Responsibility for scenery and props, and photocopying.

- First Aid person.

You also need a group of people who are committed to pray for the club. Any members of this group who are not involved in the club must be kept properly informed.

Legal Requirements

It is important that all team members are aware of current legislation regarding the care of children. In the UK this is covered by The Children Act 1989. The following need to be taken into account:

- Registration. If the club runs for more than two hours (excluding preparation and clean up time) and takes place on more than six days in the year you will need to register with your Local Authority. If in doubt check with the Day Care Advisor at your local Social Services Department.

- Premises need to be warm, adequately lit and ventilated, with sufficient lavatories and wash hand basins (the ideal is one for every ten children).

- Be realistic about the number of children you can fit in and do not overcrowd your meeting area.

- First Aid. All team members should know where to find the First Aid Box and there should be a designated team member who has done a recognised First Aid course.

- Any accident or other incident should be recorded in the Accident Book. A record should be made of the date, time, who was present, and treatment given. The record must be signed. A parent/guardian must be informed.

- Safety. All team members should know what to do in an emergency and the location of the emergency exits.

- Insurance. Check that the club is covered for public liability by your church's insurance policy.

- Recruitment of leaders. Follow your church's Child Protection Policy. All leaders should fill in and sign a confidential declaration stating whether they have been the subject of criminal or civil proceedings and whether they have caused harm to any child or put them at risk. In the UK this is required by law. (A sample form can be obtained by email from sales@tntministries.org.uk.) They should also provide the names of two people who will give a personal reference and both these should be followed up. Because allegations of abuse are often made some time afterwards these need to be retained for seven years.

- Leader/child ratios. There should be a minimum of one leader for every eight children and every small group should have two leaders. Where possible the gender of the leaders should reflect the nature of the group. If there are boys in the group there should, where possible, be a male leader present. Any group containing girls must always have a female leader present.

- A register should be kept of everyone present, leaders as well as children, which needs to be retained for seven years.

Groups

Each age range should be split into small groups of approximately ten children. Each small group requires two leaders, at least one of which should be female. The small groups are given names associated with the theme of the club, e.g. names associated with the book of Acts, such as Parthians, Medes, Elamites, Mesopotamians, Judeans, Cappadocians, Samaritans, Ethiopians, Egyptians, Romans, Cretans etc. Leaders and children wear name badges with the name of their group and the group home-base needs to be similarly identified. The group home-base is where the group meets on arrival and where Bible time occurs.

Planning the Programme

Allocate timings for all the components of the programme, making sure that adequate time is given for the Bible teaching slot. Choose other activities to fit the time remaining and remember to include the time taken to move between activities. Choose songs that reinforce the main teaching point of the session. Songs should be photocopied onto acetates or displayed on a data projector so that the words can be clearly seen by all the children. Check your church's CCL copyright licence to make sure the club is covered. (If using a video this must also be covered by the licence.)

Decide what to use as a signal for the programme to begin. It is also helpful to have a club word and associated action to call the children to attention. This could be 'witness'. When they hear this word they are to stop what they are doing, stand up and hold both hands in front of them as if reading from a Bible.

Decide how the children will be dismissed at the end. This is better done one small group at a time so that Security can check that the children are met by an adult.

Suggested daily programme

The times given are approximate and will need to be altered to fit the local situation.

- Before club starts - team prayers and final preparation.   45 mins

- Children arrive - registration, to small groups for start-up activity.   10 mins

- Up front for welcome, singing, memory verse teaching, prayer, warm-up .   20 mins

- Bible time and fun sheets in small groups.
                                                                    30 mins

- Craft activity or quiz.   15 mins

- Refreshments.   15 mins

- Games to reinforce Bible teaching.   30 mins

(If space limited, 5-7s do craft, etc. whilst the 8-11s do games. Groups swap activities for the final 30 minutes.)

- Up front for singing, memory verse revision, wind-up, prayer and dismissal.   15 mins

- Team review after children have gone home.

The Venue

If possible the meeting area should be set up as an immigration hall or border control post, possibly with many different flags from various countries to give an international feel. The registration desks are the visa application desks and are situated at the entrance to the room. The small groups take place in 'interview rooms', which should be indicated by an appropriate sign but should not be cordoned off in any way. You need a presentation area with an OHP and screen and sufficient space for puppet or drama presentations. You will also need two pin boards for the quiz and some of the warm ups. The puppets can operate from behind the pin boards covered with a sheet to hide the puppeteers. The presentation area could be labelled 'Border Control' and the games area labelled 'Health Control' and refreshments are served from 'Customs'.

Each small group requires a resource box containing scissors, glue sticks, colouring pens, biros, sticky tape and split pin paper fasteners. These should be clearly labelled with the group names. A secure storage area is required for the games equipment, resource boxes and craft equipment.

Registration

The registration desk(s) should be sited at the entrance to the club, the number required being dependent on the number of children attending. If more than one desk is in operation each desk should be clearly labelled alphabetically, e.g. A-M & N-Z. Each child requires a passport (see page 9), which acts as their entry ticket each session. The passports are kept on the desk in a box in alphabetical order. On arrival Security directs the children to the appropriate desk. Their passport is marked for that day and given to the children to take to their immigration officers (small group leaders). For the first session you will need some helpers to escort the children to their group areas to meet their leaders. The passports are handed to the immigration officers and act as a register for that session. (A master register of all children and adults present must be made at some point in the session.)

Any child arriving without a passport is directed to the Enquiry Desk ('Passport Control') where a master list of all children registered and blank passports are kept.

Advertising the Club

All your advertising materials should be attractive and look professional. They must state clearly where and when the club will take place, how long it will last and for which age groups. Parents need to know what sort of activities are on offer and that the children will be taught the Bible. Also include a contact name and telephone number and how to enrol children for the club. If a financial contribution is required this must be clearly stated. You need posters for local schools and church notice boards and leaflets to hand out.

As well as details of the club, the leaflets should include a form to fill in and return in order to enrol each child. This should state the child's name, address, telephone number, date of birth, gender, details of known conditions/allergies, contact number for parents in case of emergency, and name and telephone number of family doctor. If children will be taken off site for any reason a parent/guardian must give signed consent.

Finance

Running a successful club costs money. You will need to budget for advertising, craft materials, stationary, photocopying, games equipment, a First Aid Box and refreshments. A decision must be made about whether the children should pay a small subscription and, if so, how this will be collected.

Follow-Up

This needs to be planned in advance. Talk through how new children will be integrated into the Sunday work with a church leader. Parents enjoy seeing what their children have done, so organise a social activity at the end of the club with a meal or light refreshments and an opportunity for the children to show what they have learned.

Start-up Activities

There is normally a short period of time during which the children are arriving at the club. It is preferable for them to go straight into an activity and suggestions for these can be found on page 50.

Bible Time

This is the time set aside for teaching the Bible lesson. The lesson notes contain a commentary on the Bible passage to help the teacher understand it. Further help in lesson preparation can be found on page 10.

Visual Aids

Suggestions for these are made in the lesson material. Further help can be got from a variety of visuals and books available from your local Christian retailer. There is a visual aid on page 79 which will help explain the gospel to a child.

Fun Sheets

Each lesson contains a set of activity sheets for both age groups. These reinforce some of the Bible teaching and should be used at the end of the Bible lesson. The younger age group spans a wide ability range and some of the children may only have rudimentary reading skills. This means that some children will require more help than others.

Craft Activities

Supplementary craft activities have been provided for both age groups and can be found towards the end of the book.

Introducing and reinforcing the Bible lesson

In this book we have outlined three supplementary activities - the Warm-up, the Consolidation and the Wind-up. Though this is only one model of an integrated teaching approach, it has been used by TnT Ministries with great success for many years. We have found consistently that with this kind of repetition even the smallest child can learn big things about God.

A Warm Up is a short activity or presentation designed to arrest the attention of the children and prepare them for the Bible teaching which is to follow.

Consolidations are constructive games or activities designed to reinforce the key concepts, theme, aim or details of the Bible story that has just been taught. They generally involve plenty of physical activity and some simple equipment.

A Wind Up is the final summation of the days teaching. It involves linking the warm-up, the Bible story and the consolidation together, emphasising the central teaching point.

Warm-ups and wind-ups take around 5 minutes and a consolidation game 15-25 minutes. The ideas and suggestions are only guidelines for you to adapt and change in line with the age, number and needs of your children and limitations of your meeting space. (Further ideas can be found in the series *The Game Is Up*, published by Christian Focus Publications.)

In some warm-ups the leader demonstrates negative qualities, such as favouritism. When acting out of character we suggest that you don a hat or jacket, or call yourself a different name, so that the younger children do not equate the bad points with the leader.

Memory Verse Teaching

Learning Bible verses involves repetition; the teacher's job is to make that repetition enjoyable. This can be done in the following ways:

- Break the verse down into words or short phrases plus reference, e.g. The Lord / alone / is God. / 1 Kings 18 verse 39. Divide the children into sufficient groups to give each group a section of the verse. The groups say their word/ phrase in order and as they do so they throw their arms into the air and down again like a Mexican wave. After the verse has been said in this way two or three times reallocate the words/ phrases and start again.

- Divide the Bible verse into two sections and the children into two groups. Group A says the first half of the verse followed by the group B saying the second half. Both groups join together to say the reference. Repeat with group B saying the first half of the verse and group A saying the second. This can also be done by dividing the group into boys and girls or leaders and children.

- Chant the Bible verse, keeping time with slapping thighs twice, clapping hands twice, slapping thighs twice, clapping hands twice, etc.

- Learn actions to the words and repeat the Bible verse using the actions.

- Write the words of the Bible verse onto inflated balloons. Ask for volunteers to come out and hold up the balloons so that the audience can see the words. Repeat the verse twice then ask one of the children to burst a balloon. Repeat the verse then burst another balloon. Continue until all the balloons have been burst. For long verses you might want to burst more than one balloon at a time.

- Set the Bible verse to music. Where possible use tunes that the children already know, such as nursery rhymes.

Ensure that the children understand the meaning of the verse before teaching it.

Quizzes

These are a useful way to revise what has been learned from the Bible story and may be used instead of the craft activity. Instructions for running a quiz along with suggestions for scoring can be found on page 71.

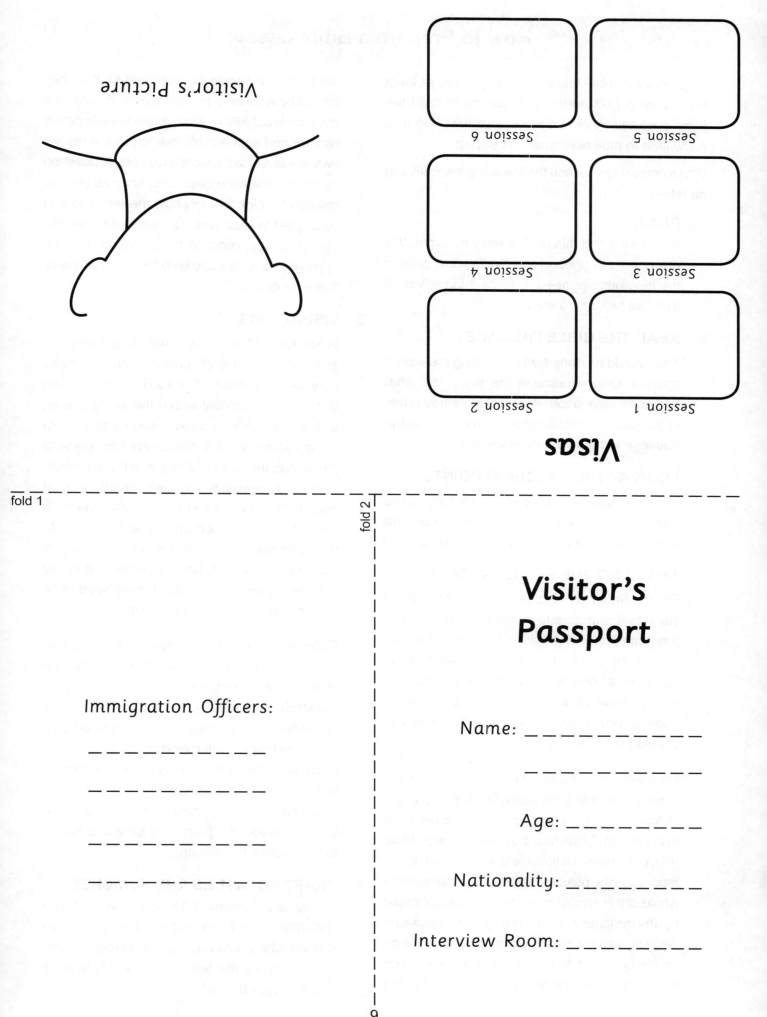

How to Prepare a Bible Lesson

To prepare a Bible lesson properly takes at least one evening (2-3 hours). It is helpful to read the Bible passage several days before teaching it to allow time to mull over what it is saying.

When preparing a lesson the following steps should be taken -

1. **PRAY!**

   In a busy world this is very easy to forget. We are unable to understand God's word without his help and we need to remind ourselves of that fact before we start.

2. **READ THE BIBLE PASSAGE**

   This should be done *before* reading the lesson manual. Our resource is the Bible, not what someone says about it. The Bible study notes in the lesson manual are a commentary on the passage to help you understand it.

3. **LOOK AT THE TEACHING POINTS**

   These should reflect the main teaching of the passage. Plan how that can be packaged appropriately for the age group you teach.

4. **TEACHING THE BIBLE PASSAGE**

   For the under 8s, decide how to tell the Bible story. Is it appropriate to recapitulate on what has happened in previous lessons? Will you involve the children in the presentation of the story? What sort of questions are appropriate to use? How will you ascertain what has been understood? Is there anything in the story that should be applied to their lives?

   For the older children this should take place in the context of simple Bible study. Do ensure that the children use the same version of the Bible. Prior to the lesson decide how the passage will be read, (e.g. one verse at a time), and who should do the reading. Is the passage short enough to read the whole of it or should some parts be paraphrased by the teacher? Work through the passage, deciding which points should be raised. Design simple questions to bring out the main teaching of the passage. The first questions should elicit the facts and should be designed so that they cannot be answered by a simple 'no' or 'yes'. If a child reads out a Bible verse as the answer, praise him/her and then ask him/her to put it in his/her own words. Once the facts have been established go on to application questions, encouraging the children to think through how the teaching can be applied to their lives. Do remember that this age group can know all the answers - it is the application of their Bible knowledge to behaviour that is so difficult!

5. **VISUAL AIDS**

   What type of visual aid will help bring the story alive for the children? Simple pictures may be appropriate. For stories where there is a lot of movement within the same scene, a flannelgraph is a good resource to use. In stories where there is movement from place to place. e.g. the story of Philip and the Ethiopian Eunuch (Lesson 5), models or pictures of people that have been cut out and made to be self-standing (perhaps by gluing them to a simple cardboard tube) is a helpful way of showing movement. Do remember that visual aids take time to make and this will need to be built into your lesson preparation.

   Pictures are very rarely required for the older age group. A Bible Time Line is useful so that the children can see where the Bible passage they are studying comes in the big picture of God's revelation to his people (see pages 80-81). Maps are helpful to demonstrate distances, etc. Pictures and models are only required for topics such as the Tabernacle, where it is difficult to visualise what is happening from reading the Bible passage. A flip-chart or similar is handy to summarise the lesson.

6. **CRAFT ACTIVITIES AND FUN SHEETS**

   These are designed to help the children understand and remember what they have learned. Many of the craft activities require prior preparation by the teacher so do not leave it until the night before!

Message Unstoppable: Acts

This series starts with Jesus' ascension and looks at his promise to his disciples in Acts 1:8. The remaining lessons show how this started to be fulfilled in the beginning chapters of Acts. The Acts of the Apostles was written by Luke (Acts 1:1, Luke 1:3), who was one of Paul's companions (Acts 16:6-10, etc. - the text changes from 'they' (Acts 16:4) to 'we').

In the first lesson Jesus promises the power of his Holy Spirit to his disciples, so that they would be witnesses for him throughout the world. The second lesson deals with the keeping of that promise and the change that comes over the disciples as a result. Peter preaches the gospel to the crowd that had gathered in Jerusalem from various nations to celebrate the Feast of Pentecost. The gift of tongues (other languages) meant that already people were hearing the good news about Jesus in their own language.

In the third lesson we see what happens to the new church in Jerusalem and how it continues to grow in spite of opposition. The Jewish authorities try to prevent the gospel spreading, even putting the apostles into prison, but to no avail. The fourth lesson looks at the increase in opposition to the gospel which culminates in the stoning of Stephen. At this point persecution breaks out in Jerusalem causing the believers to be thrust out of Jerusalem into Judea and Samaria. Jesus' promise in Acts 1:8 is starting to be fulfilled.

On the fifth day we look at Philip taking the gospel to Jews throughout Samaria and to the Ethiopian, a Jewish proselyte. The final lesson concentrates on the mission to the Gentiles, with Peter taking the gospel to Cornelius (Acts 10:1-48).

It is important for the children to realise that Jesus' command to his followers to preach repentance and forgiveness of sins in his name applies to us also (Luke 24:46-49). It is very easy for this age group to see their faith as an academic exercise that has very little relevance to everyday life. Like us, they need to be encouraged to put their faith into practice and to tell their friends about Jesus.

Series aims

1. To look at the way the gospel spread out from Jerusalem to the 'ends of the earth', and to discover the different ways God brought this about.

2. To recognise that nothing can prevent the gospel spreading - will you be part of it or will you try to stand against it?

3. To understand the importance of telling others about Jesus.

11

Teaching Points

Lesson 1   **The Great Commission**   Acts 1:1-11
The gospel is for all nations.
The Holy Spirit is given to enable the preaching of the gospel.
Jesus is alive and will return.

Lesson 2   **Beginning in Jerusalem**   Acts 2:1-42
The Holy Spirit comes as promised.
The gospel is preached in Jerusalem.
People from other nations hear the gospel.

Lesson 3   **Opposition**   Acts 5:17-42
The church grows.
Jewish leaders are jealous.
Imprisonment cannot stop the gospel.
Jewish authorities cannot stop the gospel.

Lesson 4   **Persecution**   Acts 6:7-8:3
Two responses to the gospel - acceptance or rejection.
Opposition to the gospel claims the first martyr.
Believers are scattered into Judea and Samaria.

Lesson 5   **Into Samaria**   Acts 8:4-8,26-40
God is in control.
The gospel spreads to the Samaritans.
An Ethiopian believes.

Lesson 6   **Gentile Believers**   Acts 10:1-48
The gospel is for everyone.
The gospel is preached to Gentiles.
The Holy Spirit confirms the Gentiles' salvation.

Memory work

Lesson 1   You will be my witnesses in Jerusalem, and in all Judea and Samaria, and to the ends of the earth.   Acts 1:8 (NIV)

Lesson 2   Christ died for sins once for all, to bring you to God.   1 Peter 3:18 (NIV)

Lesson 3   Believe in the Lord Jesus and you will be saved.   Acts 16:31 (NIV)

Lesson 4   I am not ashamed of the gospel, because it is the power of God for the salvation of everyone who believes.   Romans 1:16 (NIV)

Lesson 5   God commands all people everywhere to repent.   Acts 17:30 (NIV)

Lesson 6   Review lessons 1-5

Ideas for teaching these verses in memorable ways can be found on page 70.

Message Unstoppable: Acts

Lesson 1   The Great Commission

Text   Acts 1:1-11

Teaching Points   The gospel is for all nations.
The Holy Spirit is promised to enable the preaching of the gospel.
Jesus is alive and will return.

Warm Up

Skit or puppets (see script on page 72).

Trudy begins telling a story, but is constantly interrupted by Toby who wants her to tell his favourite story instead. Trudy explains that she has prepared another story and has promised the boys and girls that she would tell them that particular story. Toby tries to persuade Trudy to break her promise. Trudy uses the opportunity to teach Toby a lesson about making promises.

In today's true story from the Bible we will see what happened when someone made a promise. Come back and tell me:

1. Who made the promise? *[Jesus - Acts 1:7-8]*

2. What was promised? *[The Holy Spirit - Acts 1:8]*

3. Where did the promise-maker go? *[To heaven - Acts 1:10-11]*

Bible Time

In the Acts of the Apostles Peter is seen as the leader of the band of disciples both before and after Pentecost (Acts 1:15-22; 2:14). Peter was also the first apostle to take the gospel to the Gentiles, (Philip was a deacon), after God had demonstrated in a dream that the Gentiles were no longer to be classed as unclean (Acts 10:27-29).

1:1-2	See Luke 1:1-4. It is not known who Theophilus was - possibly an educated Roman.
1:4-5	See Luke 24:46-49.
	The Spirit had been promised many years before (Joel 2:28-29, Ezekiel 36:24-28), and now the Scriptures were about to be fulfilled. Jesus commands them to wait for the gift the Father had promised.
1:5	See Luke 3:16.
1:6	The disciples could be referring to an earthly kingdom and freedom from Roman oppression, or to the end of the age (see Matthew 24:3).
1:8	The coming of the Holy Spirit would give the disciples power to be Jesus' witnesses (see Isaiah 43:1-13). Thus, through the disciples, he continues Jesus' work on earth.
1:9	A cloud signified the glory of God in Exodus 40:34 and 1 Kings 8:10-11.

Synopsis

After his resurrection from the dead Jesus spends forty days with his disciples convincing them that he is truly alive. The disciples are concerned about the establishment of God's Kingdom, but Jesus tells them to wait in Jerusalem until he sends the Holy Spirit whom God has promised will come. The Holy Spirit will empower them to be witnesses for Jesus, starting in Jerusalem, but also expanding outwards to the province of Judea, neighbouring countries like Samaria and also to the farthest places on earth.

Visual aids

Pictures or flannelgraph of the characters you wish to use from the story including a hill as a background, two angels and a large cloud. Visual aids are also available on pages 85-93.

Map of the area - see page 15.

Fun Sheets

5-7s	Photocopy pages 16 and 17 back to back for each child.
8-11s	Photocopy pages 18 and 19 back to back for each child.

Consolidation

Game 1: Divide the children into their various small group teams. Let them sit with the group leaders in circles scattered around the play area. You will require a wrapped parcel per group. Each parcel consists of multiple layers of wrapping paper as in the traditional "pass the parcel" game - newspaper as a wrapping is adequate. Each layer of wrapping paper contains either a points card or a "tongue of fire" cut from orange paper. The points cards have random values e.g. 10, 20, 5 and some even have negative values e.g. -10, -50 etc. Tongues of fire have a very high value relative to the other points cards e.g. 200 points. These points cards and tongues of fire are placed randomly in each layer of the parcels.

When the game commences all the parcels are in a central place. At the signal, leader calling out "power", each team sends a representative to collect a parcel from the pile. Upon return, they unwrap a *single* layer of the parcel to reveal their points for that round. The parcels are then returned to the central point ready for the next round.

A large scorecard with concentric circles labelled from the middle, 'Jerusalem', 'Judea', 'Samaria' and 'ends of the earth' is used to show the various teams' progress. Markers representing each team start in the middle and progress outwards to the next concentric circle in turn with every tongue of fire received.

Points per team are tallied separately, but do not allow the team to advance - only receipt of a tongue of fire advances the team. The winning team is the one who makes it to the 'ends of the earth' zone and has the highest points.

Game 2: Divide the playing area into four zones labelled, 'Jerusalem', 'Judea', 'Samaria' and 'ends of the earth'. Divide the children into equal teams of mixed ages with no more than eight in each team. Each team must have one member in 'Jerusalem', four/five members in Judea and one/two members in Samaria. Each Jerusalem team member receives an envelope with 'The Good News' written on it and containing the memory verse written out, one word per piece of paper, "You / will / be / my/ witnesses / in / Jerusalem, / and / in / all / Judea / and / Samaria, / and / to / the / ends / of / the / earth / Acts 1:8." Make sure the memory verse papers are shuffled so that they are in random order. If possible each team's memory verse should be on a different colour paper.

At the signal the team member in Jerusalem runs to his team in Judea where the envelope is opened. The pieces of paper are then relayed one by one to the rest of the team in Samaria. This is done by one team member at a time taking only one piece of paper at a time across to Samaria, leaving it behind with the team there and returning to Judea. Team members in Judea take turns to get the pieces of paper across and only once all the pieces have arrived safely in Samaria may all the team members move across from Judea to Samaria.

Once everyone is in Samaria the entire process is repeated to get the pieces of paper to the 'ends of the earth' where the verse is finally unscrambled and laid out in order. The first team to complete the task wins.

Wind Up

Remind the children of the warm up and go over the answers to the questions. Point out that just as in Game 1 when the team could only move out from Jerusalem once they had received the tongue of fire, so too the disciples could only be Jesus' witnesses once they had received the Holy Spirit which Jesus promised he would send. Speak about the great anticipation felt as they waited for the gift to come each time and the excitement when they discovered it was a tongue of fire.

Link the way in which the message was moved from area to area in Game 2 to the way in which the good news about Jesus would spread as the disciples went further and further from Jerusalem telling people about Jesus and all that he had done by dying on the cross and rising again. Revise the memory verse.

Palestine during the time of the early church

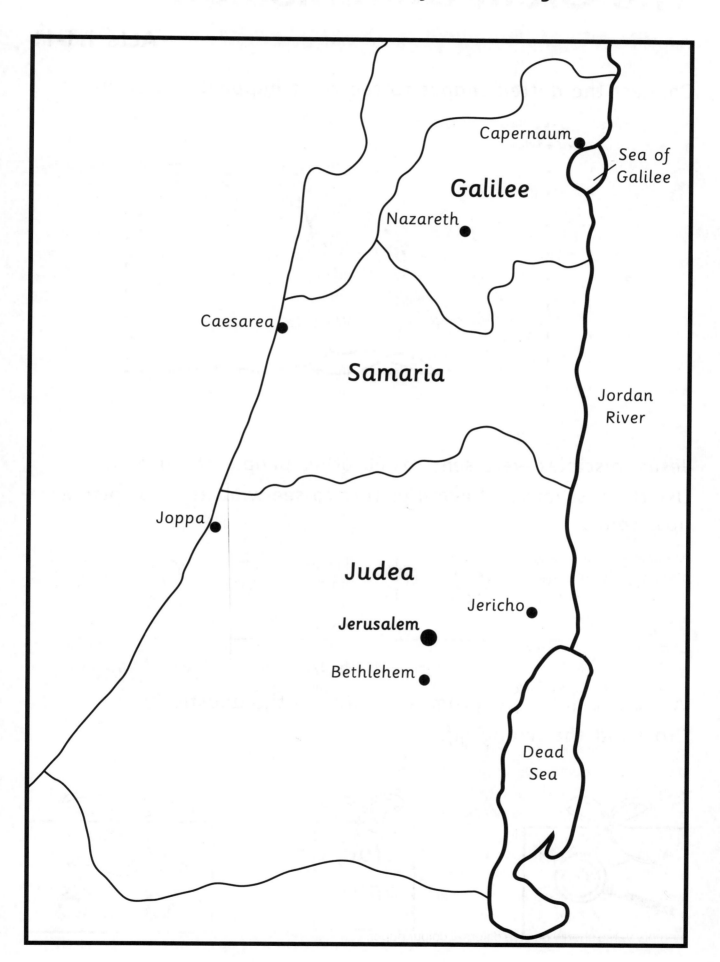

The Great Commission

Acts 1:1-11

Connect the dotted shapes to see what happened to Jesus.

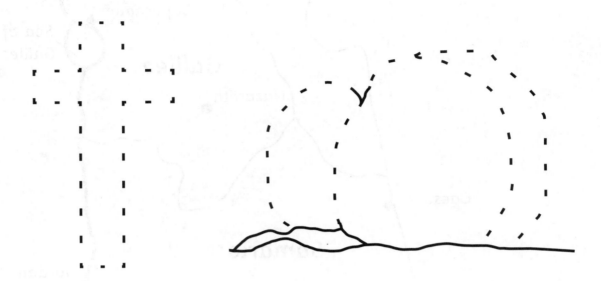

Jesus' disciples were sent to tell other people about him.
Use the first letter of every picture to see what the disciples were now called.

__ __ __ __ __ __ __ __

What gift did Jesus promise to give to the apostles?
Cross out the wrong gifts.

16

What will the apostles be able to do when they get the Holy Spirit?
Write down every second letter to find the answer.

r w e i a t d n y e a s n s

___ ___ ___ ___ ___ ___ ___ ___ ___

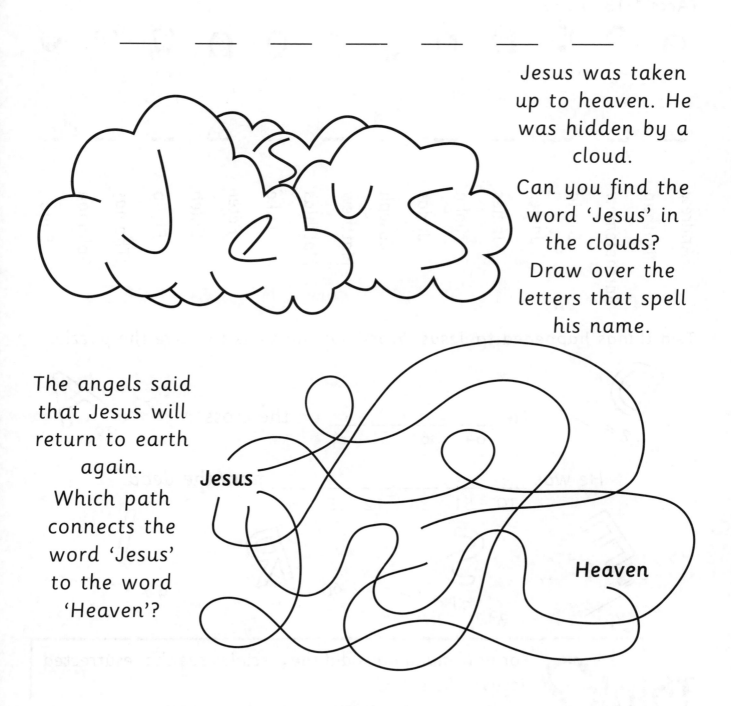

Jesus was taken up to heaven. He was hidden by a cloud.
Can you find the word 'Jesus' in the clouds? Draw over the letters that spell his name.

The angels said that Jesus will return to earth again.
Which path connects the word 'Jesus' to the word 'Heaven'?

Jesus

Heaven

Cross out all the wrong words in the memory verse: Acts 1:8

You will be my **chocolates / witnesses / cars** in Jerusalem, and in all **England / America / Judea** and Samaria, and to the **beginning / middle / ends** of the **earth / raisins / milk.**

The Great Commission

Acts 1:1-11

Draw a line from each disciple to one of the disciple's names
(Acts 1:13; 1:26)

Andrew   Nathan   Bartholomew   David   James   James   John   Judas   Joseph   Matthew   Matthias   Luke   Peter   Caleb   Philip   Thomas   Solomon   Simon

Two things happened to Jesus. Work out the sums to solve the puzzle.

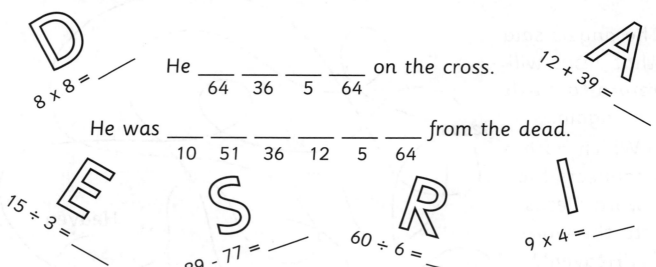

D
8 x 8 =

He ___ ___ ___ ___ on the cross.
    64 36 5 64

A
12 + 39 =

He was ___ ___ ___ ___ ___ ___ from the dead.
    10 51 36 12 5 64

E
15 ÷ 3 =

S
89 - 77 =

R
60 ÷ 6 =

I
9 x 4 =

Think Spot?

For how many days did the disciples see the resurrected Jesus? (Acts 1:3)

Jesus said he would give the disciples a gift (Acts 1:4-5).
What was the gift?

Use the words from the cloud to fill in the grid below. You will discover what Jesus asked the disciples to do. Colour in the map.

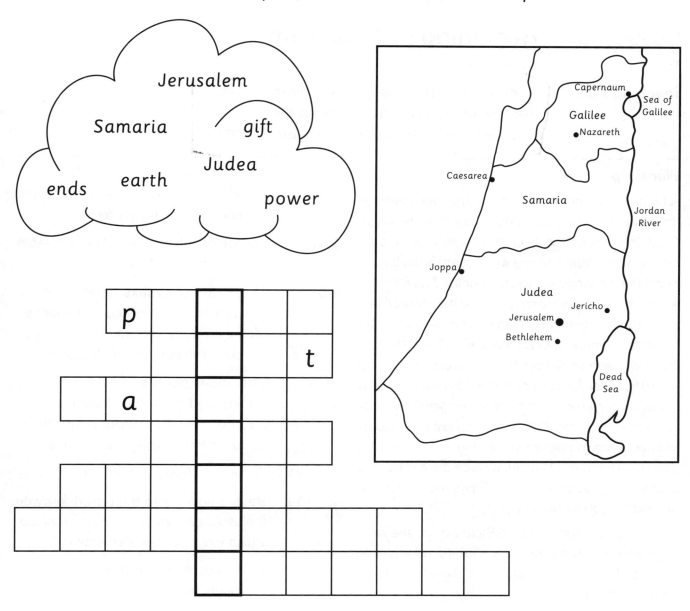

Jesus' disciples were **sent to tell other people about Jesus**. To find out what these disciples were called, cross out every second block of letters.

a p	o p	o s	o s	t l	t r	e s	e y

What does 'witness' mean?

When is it difficult to believe a promise?

Did Jesus keep his promise to the disciples? (Acts 2:4)

Message Unstoppable: Acts

Lesson 2   Beginning in Jerusalem

Text   Acts 2:1-42

Teaching Points   The Holy Spirit comes as promised.
The gospel is preached in Jerusalem.
People from other nations hear the gospel.

Warm Up

A leader, dressed in a scholarly manner (perhaps an academic gown), introduces herself as Miss Lyn Guist, the famous translator of all languages. She will be testing the teams to see which team is the best at matching the language to the country. She refers to a large political world map which all the children can see. (You may want to use an OHP or data projector to display a large map on the wall). Miss Lyn Guist then calls representatives from each group to collect a card from her. Each card contains the words, 'Jesus Christ' written in one of various languages. The cards can be found on page 76. The representative returns to their group to discuss where the card should be placed on the map. They then place the card on the country they believe it to be. This process can be repeated if you have enough cards.

In today's true story from the Bible we will see what happened when the promise that Jesus made to his disciples about the Holy Spirit came true. Come back and tell me:

1. Who spoke different languages? *[The disciples – Acts 2:4-6]*

2. Who made it happen? *[The Holy Spirit – Acts 2:4]*

3. Who heard the message? *[Many religious Jews from various countries in the world – Acts 2:5]*

Bible Time

As you teach this lesson highlight that everything happened just as Jesus promised - the Holy Spirit came, the disciples witnessed, people from the ends of the earth were gathered in Jerusalem to hear, the gospel spread.

2:1   Pentecost occurred fifty days after the Passover. It was also called the Feast of Weeks (Leviticus 23:15-22, Deuteronomy 16:9-12) and took place at the end of the barley harvest.

2:4   The other tongues were recognisable languages - cf. v.7-11.

2:5   The Feast of Weeks celebrated the anniversary of the giving of the law on Mount Sinai, so was an occasion when devout Jews gathered in Jerusalem.

2:13   The local people would not have understood what the disciples were saying, as they would not have understood the foreign languages.

2:17-21   Cf. Joel 2:28-32.

2:14-39   Peter's address to the crowd followed the usual pattern of apostolic teaching, which included four elements -

1. A recounting of the ministry and death of Jesus.

2. The resurrection - God's attestation that Jesus was the Messiah.

3. The use of OT verses to demonstrate that Jesus was the Messiah.

4. A call to repent and believe.

Note the change in Peter from before Pentecost - no longer is he locked away in a room and afraid.

2:23   Peter stresses that everything that happened was due to the plan and foreknowledge of God. 'You, with the help of wicked men ...' - both Jew and Gentile were responsible for Jesus' death.

Peter now understands what he failed to understand in Matthew 16:21-23.

2:25-28 Cf. Psalm 16:8-11.

2:34-35 Cf. Psalm 110:1.

2:39   Note that the promise is for Jews (you and your children) and for Gentiles (all those who are far off).

At the end of the session refer back to Acts 1:8. Where has the gospel spread so far?

Synopsis

While Jesus' disciples are gathered together on the day of Pentecost the Holy Spirit comes just as Jesus promised. The coming of the Spirit is audible and visible and he enables the disciples to speak foreign languages. The disciples are accused of being drunk (due to their strange speech) but Peter, now empowered by the Spirit and no longer timid and afraid, boldly proclaims the death and resurrection of Jesus as proof that Jesus is in fact the Christ. When asked how they should respond to this news Peter tells them to repent and be baptised.

Visual aids

Pictures or flannelgraph. You need a group of disciples and Peter. In either case you need to be able to add the flames at the appropriate point in the story. Younger children can be asked to blow to make the sound of the wind. Visual aids can be found on pages 85-93.

Map of the area - see page 15.

To demonstrate the work of the Holy Spirit, wave a floppy glove around. Explain that we are all like this floppy glove when it comes to doing God's work. We cannot do anything on our own, but when someone is filled with the Holy Spirit, (put your hand in the glove), God can make him or her really useful.

Fun Sheets

5-7s   Photocopy pages 22 and 23 back to back for each child.

8-11s   Photocopy pages 24 and 25 back to back for each child.

Consolidation

Game 1: This is a scavenger hunt where the children will gather items that represent the content of Peter's speech on the day of Pentecost. Divide the children into equal teams of mixed age groups with no more than eight in each team. Each team is given the task list found on page 77. At the signal, the team members work in pairs to find the items on the task list. The first team to complete the tasks and return to a leader designated as 'Peter' who will check the items, is the winning team. If the items listed are too easily available or not available at all, depending on your environment, then you may wish to create your own specific items that the children need to find and hide these around your play area. You could also simply use drawings of the items on cards and hide the cards.

Game 2: All the children line up in the middle of the play area. When the leader calls out 'sin', the children walk towards one end of the play area marked 'sin'. While the children are walking the leader calls out, 'repent' at which point the children need to turn around and run towards the opposite end of the play area. Mark off a safe zone at that end. At each round, the last few children to cross the line/rope/touch the wall on the safe side are eliminated. The winners are the last two/three left over. One may want to play this game according to age groups. You may also want to call out 'sin' while the children are running towards the safe zone in which case they need to turn and start walking away from the safe zone. Try to make the calling as unpredictable as possible forcing the children to listen carefully.

Wind Up

Remind the children of the warm up and review the questions. Point out that the Holy Spirit came as promised and the gospel was preached. The first game gives the children a good way of bringing to mind what Peter preached about: Peter taught the Jewish people about the good news of Jesus when he explained that Jesus had to die (hold up the sticks as a cross) and rise again (stone) etc. The second game reinforces the idea of repentance as being a turning away from sin and trusting in Jesus. Many, many people heard about the good news of Jesus Christ when Peter spoke on that day. About 3000 of them turned to God and trusted in Jesus. Revise the memory verse.

Beginning in Jerusalem

Acts 2:1-42

Can you number these pictures in the right order? (v1-4)

Where were the disciples when they received the gift of the Holy Spirit? (Check the correct box)

[ ] Judea [ ] Samaria [ ] Jerusalem

What did the Holy Spirit help the disciples to do?
Crack the code to discover the answer.

◎	★	✴	✴	☼	⊞	⊕	◇	☆	✪	回
a	b	d	e	G	k	o	p	s	t	u

___ ___ ___ ___ ___   ___ ___ ___ ___ ___   ___ ___ ___

22

The people heard the disciples telling about the wonders of God in their own languages. (Colour all the matching speech shapes to see who is speaking the same language. See if anyone in your group can speak one or more of these languages!)

Colour the blocks marked 'b' to uncover an important message.

b	m	a	n	y	b	p	e	o	p	l	e	b	b	b	b
c	o	u	l	d	b	u	n	d	e	r	s	t	a	n	d
b	b	t	h	e	b	b	g	o	o	d	b	n	e	w	s
b	o	f	b	J	e	s	u	s	b	C	h	r	i	s	t

Peter told the people what they should do.
(Colour the correct answers).

repent   listen   believe   teach

Beginning in Jerusalem

Acts 2:1-42

What happened after the disciples received the Holy Spirit?
(To discover the answer find twelve words listed at the side of the word search. Each word reads in a straight line horizontally, vertically or diagonally).

H	l	a	n	g	u	a	g	e	s
o	p	t	o	n	g	u	e	s	p
l	J	e	r	u	s	a	l	e	m
y	P	f	n	e	t	d	k	e	r
S	e	i	a	t	e	a	G	o	d
p	t	r	d	z	e	d	r	n	e
i	e	e	a	p	s	c	i	s	s
r	r	m	s	t	e	w	o	d	t
i	a	h	c	e	c	r	o	s	w
t	d	a	s	o	u	n	d	.	t

acts
amazed
fire
God
Holy Spirit
Jerusalem
languages
pentecost
Peter
sound
speak
tongues
wind

Now starting from the top and reading from left to right, write down the remaining letters in the spaces below.

___ ___ ___ ___ ___ ___   ___ ___ ___ ___ ___ ___ ___ ___ ___

___ ___ ___ ___   ___ ___ ___ ___ ___ ___

How had Jesus kept his promise?

How do we know that the 'tongues' were recognizable languages? (Acts 2:11)

Think Spot?

24

Crack the code to find the memory verse: 1 Peter 3:18

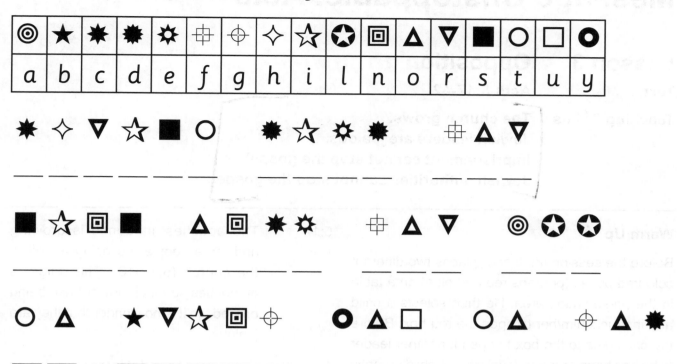

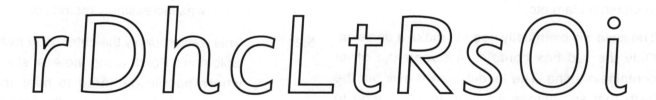

_ _ _ _ _ _   _ _ _ _   _ _ _

_ _ _ _   _ _ _ _   _ _ _   _ _ _

_ _   _ _ _ _ _ _   _ _ _   _ _   _ _ _

_ _ _ _ _ _ _   _ _ _   _ _ _ _ _ _

The strange word below is actually two words that describe who Jesus is (one in uppercase and the other in lowercase). They're also jumbled up! See if you can unscramble them and write the two words below the puzzle.

rDhcLtRsOi

Jesus is both ____ ____ ____ ____ and

___ ___ ___ ___ ___ ___

(Acts 2:36)

When the crowd understood Peter's speech, they were very concerned. What did Peter tell them to do? (Acts 2:38)

What does that mean?

Discuss

Message Unstoppable: Acts

Lesson 3   Opposition

Text   Acts 5:17-42

Teaching Points   The church grows.
Jewish leaders are jealous.
Imprisonment cannot stop the gospel.
Jewish authorities cannot stop the gospel.

Warm Up

Before the session the leader places two different coloured boxes (perhaps red and blue) on a table in the presentation area. He then selects a child and instructs him/her to open the red box. Before the child gets to the box to open it another leader (who has been prompted) calls to the child urgently and instructs them to rather open the blue box. The two leaders then compete against each other to influence the child's decision about who they should obey and why. The one leader may say that the other is simply trying to trick the child and the other leader may appeal to their seniority on the leadership team etc.

The child will eventually need to make a decision. Only the red box contains a sweet, the other contains nothing. The leader then draws out the truth that sometimes it's hard to know who to listen to.

In today's true story from the Bible we will see what happened when some people had to choose between two different instructions. Come back and tell me:

1. Who had to choose between two instructions? *[The Apostles – Acts 5:29]*

2. What were the two instructions and who gave them? *['Tell the people the full message of this new life' – God (Acts 5:20) and 'Do not speak in the name of Jesus' – Sanhedrin (Acts 5:40)]*

3. Who did they obey? *[God – Acts 5:42]*

Bible Time

At the beginning of the session refer back to Acts 1:8. Where has the gospel spread so far?

5:17   The apostles' influence is growing and more people are being added to the church (5:12-16). The religious authorities see their power base being eroded, so it is no wonder that they are jealous.

5:18-20   Even prison cannot stop the gospel being preached! The temple was surrounded by a number of courtyards, which only ritually clean worshippers were allowed to enter (see temple plan on page 75). The courts became increasingly holy as you neared the temple and entry to them was increasingly restricted.

5:21   This was probably the outer court (with Solomon's Porch along the east side), where people gathered to hear the scribes debate and where the money changers had their stalls.

5:28   'We gave you strict orders' refers back to 4:18. The apostles are being accused of deliberately setting the people against the Sanhedrin.

5:29-32   Peter uses every opportunity to preach the gospel (see 4:8-12). The emphasis is not on the guilt of the Jewish authorities but on God's providence.

5:30   Peter refers to the crucifixion as 'hanging on a tree' (Deuteronomy 21:22-23). This makes God's exaltation of Jesus even more remarkable.

5:38-39   If it is from God it cannot be stopped.

5:41	Note the apostles' reaction - they rejoiced.
5:42	The gospel was preached in the temple courts and from house to house. The first part of Acts 1:8 is being fulfilled.

Synopsis

As the apostles' influence grows so the religious leaders become jealous and seek to silence them by putting them in jail. An angel rescues them from jail and instructs them to preach in the temple courts which they do. The religious leaders discover that they have been freed from prison and they re-arrest them and bring them before the Sanhedrin. They instruct them to stop talking about Jesus. Peter addresses them with similar content to his speech on the day of Pentecost but this just makes the religious leaders so angry that they want to put the apostles to death. They are persuaded not to do this by a Pharisee named Gamaliel. Instead they have the apostles beaten and instruct them not to speak about Jesus anymore. The apostles ignore this instruction and continue to tell everyone about Jesus.

Visual aids

Pictures or flannelgraph. You need Peter, a group of apostles, a group of priests, the High Priest and Gamaliel. Visual aids are on pages 85-93.

Map of the area - see page 15.

Fun Sheets

5-7s   Photocopy pages 28 and 29 back to back for each child.

8-11s   Photocopy pages 30 and 31 back to back for each child.

Consolidation

Game 1: At the signal, the children begin running from one side of the playing area to the other. All but one leader represent the Jewish authorities who catch the children and send them to jail (a cordoned off area). The remaining leader is an angel who allows the captured children to go free. The 'Jewish authorities' could humorously ask the children how they could be playing again if they had just been caught. The game ends after a signal from the 'Jewish authorities'.

Game 2: A relay concluded with the unscrambling of the memory verse. Split the children into equal teams of mixed age groups with no more than eight in each team. Each team should have a bag of seven inflated balloons – each balloon having a snippet of the memory verse: Believe / in the / Lord Jesus / and you / will be / saved / Acts 16:31. At the signal, one member from each team should take a balloon and run to the other end of the demarcated playing area where they need to sit on the balloon. When the balloon has burst, they are to pick up the snippet of paper (as well as the balloon pieces) and run back to his/her team. The game continues until all snippets of the memory verse have been collected. The team then unscrambles the verse and shouts it out as if they were proclaiming it to the world. The first team to shout (and have the verse in the correct order) wins! **Tip:** Inflate the balloons before the session and store them in a duvet cover to contain them and prevent them from popping. Each team should have seven of the same colour balloons to make handing them out easier.

Wind Up

The gospel is reaching many people and it cannot be stopped, not even by the authorities. The apostles chose to obey Jesus' instruction to be his witnesses to the ends of the earth and they refused to obey those who opposed the message about Jesus. The first game demonstrates the theme of opposition and rescue. The second game demonstrates the way in which the gospel message was boldly proclaimed. The apostles continued to spread God's message even though it meant risk to their lives and being imprisoned.

Opposition

In Jerusalem:

More and more people started following the apostles and believing in Jesus. Cross out all the words with the letter 'y' or 'd' in them and then write the word that is left on the lines to see how the Jewish leaders felt about what was happening.

happy   sad   jealous   angry   amazed

_____   _____   _____   _____   _____   _____   _____

Draw the apostles in jail.

At night an angel opened the doors and let the apostles out of jail.

See where they went to speak about Jesus.

Jail

Temple Courts

How did the leaders feel when they discovered that the apostles were not in jail...even with the doors locked? (v.24) Circle the face.

 Happy Angry Proud Puzzled Surprised Jealous

The leaders caught the apostles again and told them to:

☐ pay a fine
☐ stop speaking about Jesus
☐ do 50 press ups

But the apostles said that it was more important to obey God than men. This made the Jewish leaders very (v.33):

 Happy Angry Proud Puzzled Surprised Jealous

So they punished the apostles and sent them away. Instead of being sad, the apostles were rejoicing. (v.41)

Did they carry on speaking about Jesus? (v.42)

☐ No   ☐ Yes

Oh no! It looks like the e's from this memory verse have been put into jail! Let them out so that they can do what they need to do.

B _ li _ v _ in th _ Lord J _ sus and you will b _ sav _ d.

Acts 16:31

29

Opposition

In Jerusalem:

1. Many people became Christians.

2. This made the enemies of the apostles jealous and they had them put in jail.

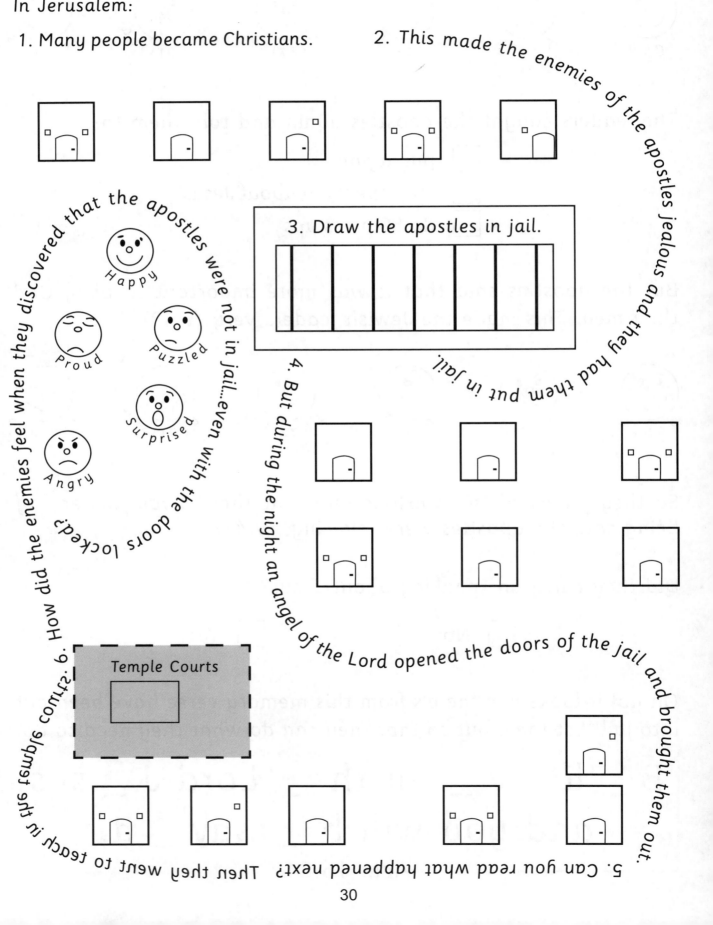

3. Draw the apostles in jail.

4. But during the night an angel of the Lord opened the doors of the jail and brought them out.

5. Can you read what happened next? Then they went to teach in the temple courts. 6. How did the enemies feel when they discovered that the apostles were not in jail...even with the doors locked?

Happy

Proud

Puzzled

Surprised

Angry

Temple Courts

Who said what?

Trace a line from the name to the correct person or group and then to what they said.

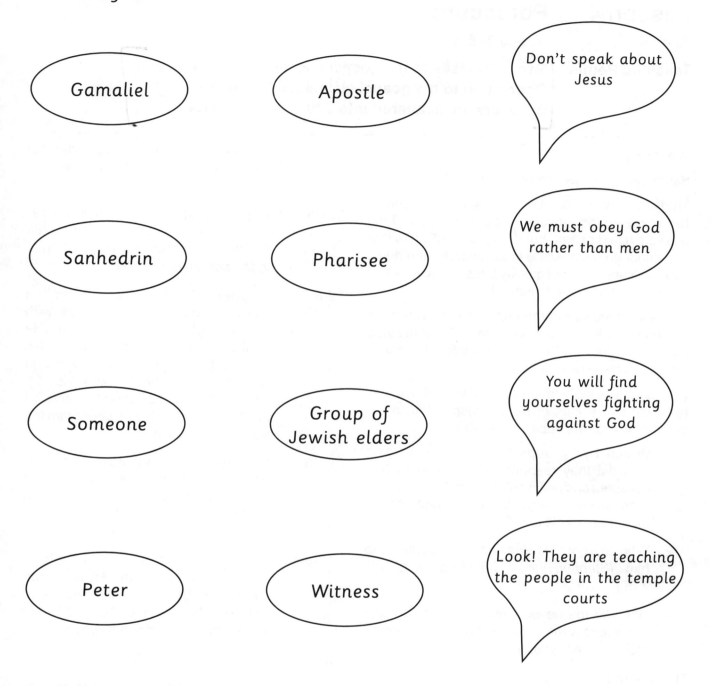

Gamaliel

Apostle

Don't speak about Jesus

Sanhedrin

Pharisee

We must obey God rather than men

Someone

Group of Jewish elders

You will find yourselves fighting against God

Peter

Witness

Look! They are teaching the people in the temple courts

The apostles went to prison and suffered because they taught everyone about Jesus. Did this put them off? (Acts 5:42)

Think Spot?

What does this story teach about what might happen to us when we talk to others about Jesus?

Message Unstoppable: Acts

Lesson 4   Persecution

Text   Acts 6:7–8:3

Teaching Points   Two responses to the gospel - acceptance or rejection.
Opposition to the gospel claims the first martyr.
Believers are scattered into Judea and Samaria.

Warm Up

Skit or puppets (see script on page 74).

Trudy is very excited because she has received two tickets to the most fantastic theme park. Toby is also excited at first, but then Trudy tells him that he cannot go because he is too short for the rides. Toby's disappointment quickly turns to jealousy and he becomes very nasty indeed.

The leader draws out the fact that sometimes the same news can be very good news for some who accept it eagerly and very bad news for others who may even become embittered.

In today's true story from the Bible we will see how two different groups of people responded to the same news. Come back and tell me:

1. Which two groups heard the news and how did they respond? *[Many priests who accepted and believed and certain synagogue members who were jealous and rejected the message – Acts 6:7, 9]*

2. Who brought the news and what happened to him? *[Stephen and he was killed – Acts 6:8, 7:60]*

3. How did the news continue to spread? *[As Christians were scattered they told everyone the news – Acts 8:4]*

Bible Time

At the beginning of the session refer back to Acts 1:8. Where has the gospel spread so far?

6:7   The church in Jerusalem continues to grow, including some priests.

6:8   Stephen was one of the seven men, 'full of the Spirit and wisdom', who had been appointed to organise the daily distribution of food (Acts 6:1-7).

6:9   Stephen preached the gospel to the Greek-speaking Jews in Jerusalem and met with opposition.

6:11   Stephen was accused of speaking out against the temple and the Law (see Acts 6:13-14).

7:2-53   Stephen's speech in his defence. (This needs to be paraphrased for the children - the lesson should concentrate on the spread of the gospel.)

7:2-8   Stephen starts by reminding his listeners about God's dealings with the father of their race, Abraham. He recalls God's call of Abraham and his promise to give Abraham a land and many descendants (Genesis 12:1-3). Abraham believed God and God entered into a covenant with him, giving him the sign of circumcision.

7:9-16   This section deals with Joseph. Joseph was rejected by his brothers, who sold him into slavery, yet he was the one whom God had provided to save his people Israel from famine.

7:17-36   Stephen then goes on to talk about Moses. Like Joseph, Moses was appointed by God as leader and deliverer of his people (Acts 7:35), yet these same people rejected him.

7:37   See Deuteronomy 18:15.

7:38-43   One of the charges brought against Stephen was that he taught that Jesus would change the Mosaic Law. Stephen reminds the Sanhedrin that when Moses gave the Law their fathers refused to obey it. The verses quoted in v.42-43 are from Amos 5:25-27.

7:44-50   The second charge against Stephen was that he spoke against the temple. In this section Stephen deals with the building of the Tabernacle and later the temple, pointing out that God does not live in houses made by human hands (see Isaiah 66:1-2).

32

7:51-53	Stephen completes his defence by turning on his accusers, stating that they are just like their fathers - they disobey God's Law and they kill the prophets that testify to the coming of Jesus.
7:58	Those who accused Stephen were responsible for carrying out the sentence.
7:60	Note that although Stephen denounced the sin (Acts 7:51-53) he was still concerned for the sinners.
8:1-4	As a result the Christians were scattered throughout Judea and Samaria and took the gospel with them.

Synopsis

As the number of converts to Christianity in Jerusalem grows so too does the opposition to the message about Jesus. One particular Jewish group falsely accuses Stephen of blasphemy and he is brought before the Sanhedrin. In his defence he provides a survey of God's dealings with his chosen people from the time of Abraham's call until the building of the temple under Solomon. He points out Israel's rebellion at various points in their history and accuses his hearers of the same hard-heartedness in their rejection of Jesus and his death. Filled with the Holy Spirit, Stephen tells of his vision of the Son of Man at the right hand of God in heaven. The leaders cannot bear to hear his words and have him stoned to death for blasphemy. That same day widespread persecution of Christians begins in Jerusalem and Christian people are scattered throughout Judea and Samaria.

Visual aids

Pictures or flannelgraph. You need two groups of people, a group of five men, Philip, Stephen, High Priest, Saul. Visual aids are available on pages 85-93.

Map of the area - see page 15.

Fun Sheets

5-7s   Photocopy pages 34 and 35 back to back for each child.

8-11s   Photocopy pages 36 and 37 back to back for each child.

Consolidation

Game: Divide the group into four mixed age teams and designate a colour per team (red, green, blue or yellow). Each team is given a pack of paper plates marked with their team colour (other suitable markers or balls can also be used). Divide the play area into different zones designated, 'Jerusalem', 'Judea', 'Samaria' and 'ends of the earth'. The game begins in 'Jerusalem'. The aim of the game is to place as many plates as possible in the different zones without being caught by the leaders, designated 'Saul' and the 'Sanhedrin'.

If a child is tagged while carrying a plate that plate is confiscated and they are sent to jail from which there is no escape. If they manage to successfully place a plate, that plate can no longer be moved and they return to Jerusalem to collect another plate. Leaders may not tag children who do not have a plate with them.

Points are awarded for each plate placed in a zone, but the zones have different values - Jerusalem is the home zone and has zero points, Judea is worth one point, Samaria two points and the 'ends of the earth' is worth five points per plate placed. The winning team is the one that has the highest score once all plates are placed and/or confiscated.

This game can be adapted to be played indoors by using buckets to designate the different zones, coloured clothing pegs as markers and by allowing only one team member to move at a time as in a relay.

Wind Up

Remind the children of the warm up and how sometimes the same news can cause two groups of people to respond in two completely different ways. Remind the children how the good news about Jesus continued to spread despite all the opposition. Help them to see that not even the death of Stephen stopped it going out. In fact it went out even further as a result of his death and the persecution of Christians. Remind the children that God is in control even when things don't seem to be going well. Revise the memory verse.

Answer for spot the difference on page 35.

33

Persecution

Acts 6:7–8:3

Circle the correct words:

- Some of the Jews were very **happy / angry** about what Stephen said.
- They secretly told people to lie about what Stephen was saying. **True / False**

Join the dots in each letter to see what Stephen spoke about in his speech.

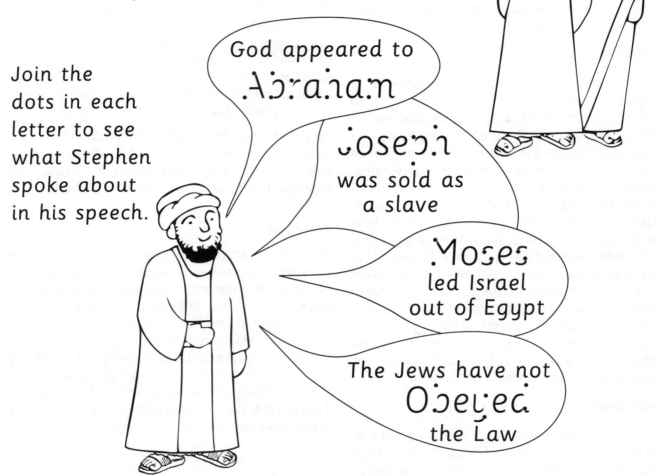

God appeared to Abraham

Joseph was sold as a slave

Moses led Israel out of Egypt

The Jews have not Obeyed the Law

Colour only the shapes with a small circle in them to discover who Stephen saw while he was speaking.

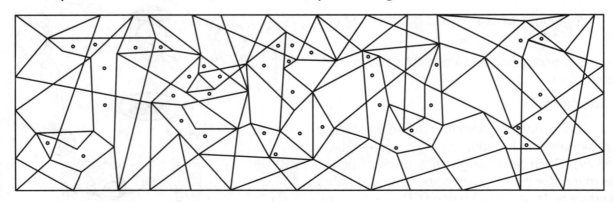

Stephen's message made some people happy and other people angry. Can you find ten differences between the pictures below? Draw circles around the differences.

After Stephen was stoned, Saul began to bully the Christians and put them in jail. Many of the Christians ran away. Using the numbered letters below, fill in the spaces to see where the Christians went to.

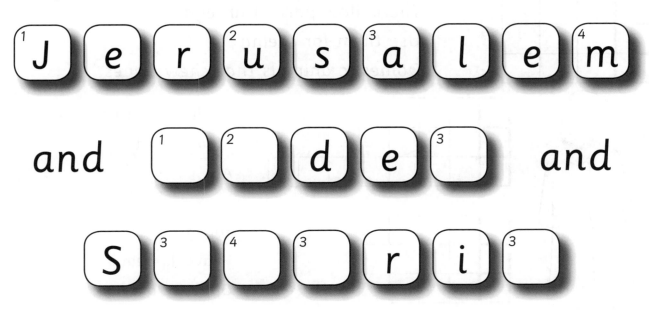

Persecution

Acts 6:7–8:3

What did Stephen do? Acts 6:8

_____ and _____

How did Stephen speak? Acts 6:10 _____

What lie was told? Acts 6:11 _____

Solve the clues and then write the answers in the boxes. When you're done, read down the first column to discover Stephen's message to the Jews.

365 days
Vegetable that will make you cry
Opposite of 'over'

Opposite of 'clean'
Presses clothes
Sun _ _ _ _ _
Opposite of 'disobey'
Straw _ _ _ _ _ or Blue _ _ _ _ _ _
Use them for hearing
The yellow part of an egg
Use them for seeing
Domestic animals that chew bones

At the end of your feet
Glad, elated
All

Young sheep
Heavenly being
Opposite of black

Stephen was stoned to death because he told the Jewish leaders the truth about Jesus. After Stephen's death a great persecution of Christians started in Jerusalem.

What does 'persecution' mean? (mark all the correct ones)
- O Being badly treated.
- O Being put in prison.
- O Suffering.

Because of the persecution, the Christians were scattered from Jerusalem. What did they do as they went out from Jerusalem? (Acts 8:4)

_____

Colour the areas on the map to show how many of the areas Jesus mentioned in Acts 1:8 have already been covered in our great adventure!

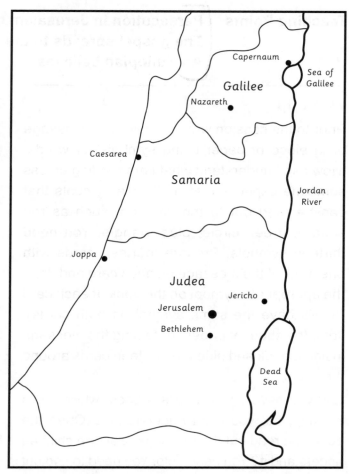

What does this story teach us about people's reaction to the good news about Jesus?

How is Jesus' command in Acts 1:8 coming true?

Who is actually in control of all that is going on?

Think Spot?

Discuss When do you find it hardest to talk to people about Jesus?

What have you learnt from this lesson to help you speak to your friends about Jesus?

Message Unstoppable: Acts

Lesson 5 ? Into Samaria

Text Acts 8:4-8, 26-40

Teaching Points Persecution in Jerusalem causes the Christians to be scattered.
The gospel spreads to the Samaritans.
An Ethiopian believes.

Warm Up

Prior to the session write the following message on a piece of paper using symbols for words: 'How can I understand what I am reading unless someone explains it to me?' Use symbols that can be read out to the children, such as red square, green circle, blue triangle. You need thirteen symbols. Prepare fourteen cards with one word of the message on each card and draw the appropriate symbol on the back of each card ('I' will have the same symbol on both cards). Tape the sheet of paper containing the message inside a book and hide the fourteen cards around the room.

Say you have come across a book, which looks exciting, but you can't understand it. Open the book and read out the message. Can the children understand it? You need help. You need to find out what the symbols mean. Ask them to search for the fourteen cards with symbols on. Once they are found read out the message and ask an older child to pin the symbols in order onto a board. Turn them over to discover the meaning.

In today's true story from the Bible someone needed to understand what he was reading:

1. Who was the man? *[An Ethiopian eunuch – Acts 8:27]*

2. What was he reading? *[Isaiah – Acts 8:28]*

3. Who helped him understand it? *[Philip – Acts 8:35]*

Bible Time

At the beginning of the session refer back to Acts 1:8. Where has the gospel spread so far?

8:4 Note the readiness of the believers to preach the gospel.

8:5 The specific city is not named.

8:6-7 The miracles that accompanied Philip's preaching to the Samaritans were similar to those that accompanied the ministry of Jesus (e.g. Mark 1:32-34) and the apostles (Acts 2:42-43; 5:12-16). It must be remembered that the Samaritans were not considered by the Jews to be Gentile, but heretics, and were hated as such. The miraculous signs demonstrated that God was at work amongst the Samaritans as well as amongst the Jews.

8:26 Philip had established the gospel in Samaria. An angel now sends him on to the road between Jerusalem and Gaza in southwest Judea. He was obedient. This is the next step towards 'the ends of the earth'.

8:27 The eunuch was possibly a God-fearing Gentile. Ethiopia was linked to Arabia and Israel by trade routes going back some 1,000 years to the time of King Solomon and the Queen of Sheba, hence he had some understanding of Jewish beliefs. The Kingdom of Ethiopia lay on the Nile between Aswan and Khartoum. 'Candace' was the dynastic title for the King's mother, who held real power. The Eunuch came from a completely different background, culture, etc. but Philip preached the same gospel to him as he did to everyone he met - the good news of Jesus.

8:28-29 The Ethiopian would have been travelling with a considerable company of people. It was not unusual for a stranger to join such a group.

8:30-31 People in those days usually read aloud. God had prepared someone to answer his questions.

8:32-35 Isaiah 53:7-8. Philip taught from the Scriptures, applying them to the Christ (as Jesus himself had done). This demonstrates the importance of knowing the Scriptures (both Old and New Testaments), so that we can lead others to Christ.

8:39 The Eunuch went on his way rejoicing - in contrast to the rich young man, who went away sorrowful (Matthew 19:22).

8:40 Azotus is about twenty miles north of Gaza. Philip then went on to Caesarea, preaching the gospel to all towns on his way. He settled in Caesarea and brought up a family (Acts 21:8-9).

Philip could have told this story to Luke, the writer of Acts, when he and Paul visited Philip in Caesarea some twenty years later (Acts 21:8).

Synopsis

After the stoning of Stephen persecution breaks out in Jerusalem and the Christians are scattered. Wherever they go they tell people the good news about Jesus. In this way the gospel even spreads to neighbouring Samaria. On one occasion Philip is instructed by an angel to travel south. On his way he meets an Ethiopian eunuch who is struggling to understand the prophecy of Isaiah which he has with him on a scroll. Philip explains the good news about Jesus from Isaiah and the Ethiopian believes and is baptised by Philip.

Visual aids

Map of the area - see page 15.

A rolled up piece of paper with the words from Isaiah written on it. You can make the document look like an ancient parchment by lightly rubbing black coffee with a piece of cotton wool over the paper and leaving it to dry before writing on it with a felt tip pen. This would make a good prop if you were to dramatise this story. There are other visual aids on pages 85-93.

Fun Sheets

5-7s   Photocopy pages 40 and 41 back to back for each child.

8-11s Photocopy pages 42 and 43 back to back for each child.

Consolidation

Game 1: This is a variation of the much loved 'shipwreck' game. Designate one section of the play area as the river and leave a number of bed sheets or large pieces of blue cloth scattered around. There should be one cloth/sheet per group and it should be large enough to cover the group when they are huddled together on the ground (with a bit of effort of course!). The leader stands in the middle of the play area and calls the following commands in random order, using each command several times. The children respond as quickly as possible. You could eliminate from the game those who respond last if you so wish.

- 'Scatter' - the children run around the play area trying to get as much distance as possible between them and the leaders who are also moving around and designated as 'persecutors'.

- 'Chariot' - the children stop whatever they are doing and get into groups of three. One person kneels with arms stretched out and slightly behind them to form a chariot. The other two children stand behind the chariot, one behind each arm of the child posing as a chariot to represent Philip and the Ethiopian.

- 'Baptism' - the children run to the river, but this time they get into their small groups and attempt to huddle together and cover themselves with the cloths. You can eliminate from the game anyone who is not covered if you wish.

Game 2: Divide the children into teams of 6-8 per team of mixed ages. The two oldest children form a 'chariot' by holding each others forearms. A young child is the Ethiopian who is carried sitting in the forearms of the 'chariot'. 'Philip' will run alongside the 'chariot' and, of course, any good chariot needs two to four horses galloping slightly ahead of the 'chariot'! Run around a designated course possibly around a few palm trees and ending at a river.

Wind Up

Remind the children about the warm-up and go over the answers to the questions. The older children should know which part of the Bible the Ethiopian was reading (Isaiah). Refer to the games and ask the following questions:

1. Why did they scatter?
2. Why did Philip get into the chariot?
3. Why did they get into the water?

Into Samaria

Acts 8:4-8, 26-40

What is the name of the man who went to Samaria to teach the people about Jesus? (Circle the correct name)

Paul   Saul   Philip

When the crowds 👤 heard 👂 him teach 📢 about Jesus ✝ and saw 👁 the miraculous signs he did ✋, they all listened carefully to what he said.

Colour red each block that DOES NOT have a picture from the story to see what the people felt while Philip was there.

👁	👁	〜	👤	👤	〜	〜	〜	✋	〜	✝	〜
👤	📢	〜	👁	📢	〜	👁	〜	📢	〜	📢	〜
✋	✝	〜	✋	👂	〜	✝	〜	👂	〜	〜	〜
〜	📢	〜	👂	✋	〜	📢	〜	✋	📢	〜	👁
〜	〜	〜	📢	👁	〜	〜	〜	👤	👁	〜	✝

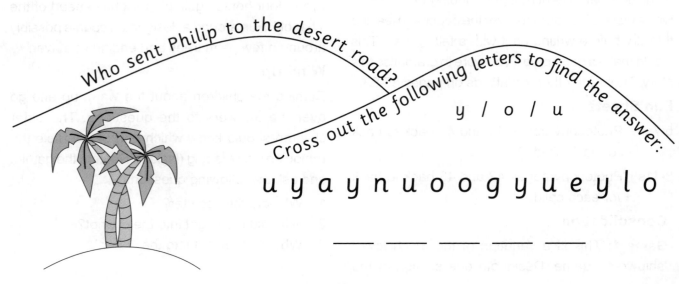

Who sent Philip to the desert road?

Cross out the following letters to find the answer: y / o / l / u

u y a y n u o o g y u e y l o

_ _ _ _ _ _

40

Join the dots to see what the Ethiopian was riding on. Can you draw a horse in the front?

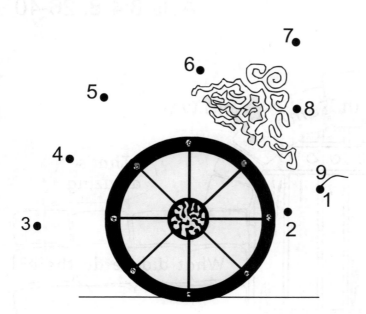

Listen to each sentence being read and circle the best picture.

1. Philip ran up to the

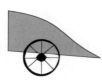  

2. The Ethiopian was reading

3. Philip spoke to him about Jesus on the

4. The Ethiopian believed. He was baptised in

Into Samaria

Acts 8:4-8, 26-40

Do the sums to discover what happened next:

They (help -lp +card -c) = _____ the message about Jesus from

(Philemon - lemon +lip) = _____ and saw

the (mirage -ge +cull -l +house -he) = _____

sip -p +g +bins -bi) = _____ he did and this made everyone

(like -ke +stem -m +nut -ut) = _____ to him.

An (ant -t +get -t +hill -hil) = _____ told Philip to go

(seek -eek +mouth -m) = _____ to the

(dead -ad serve -ve +pit -pi) = _____ road that goes down from

(Jerry -ry +you -yo +sale +man -an) = _____ to Gaza.

What does this story teach us about who needs to hear the message about Jesus?

How can you tell people from other countries about Jesus?

42

While he was on his way to the desert road Philip discovered something. Answer the questions correctly to reveal the code you must use to crack the mystery question.

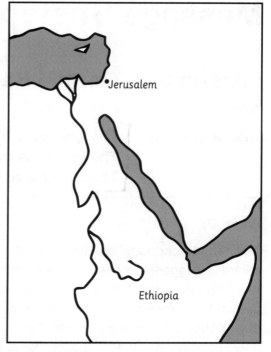

Jerusalem

Ethiopia

Clue 1:
This is where Philip's new friend came from.

___ ___ ___ ___ ___ ___ ___ ___
 2   5   4   5

Clue 2:
Where had this official been?

___ ___ ___ ___ ___ ___ ___ ___
 3   2   1   2

Clue 3:
The official was ___ ___ ___ ___ ___ ___ ___ the Scriptures on his
                  1   2   8   5

___ ___ ___ ___ ___ ___ ___
 6   1   5   4

Mystery question:
What did the Ethiopian do as he went on his way?

___ ___ ___ ___ ___ ___ ___ ___
 1   2   3   4   5   6   2   8

DiscusS

The Ethiopian needed help to understand the Scriptures. Where do you get help from to understand the Bible?

How do we know that Jesus is still in control of the way the message about him is going out all over the world?

Message Unstoppable: Acts

Lesson 6   Gentile Believers

Text   Acts 10:1-48

Teaching Point
- The gospel is for everyone.
- The gospel is preached to the Gentiles.
- The Holy Spirit confirms the Gentiles' salvation.

Warm Up

The leader chooses several people to receive awards. Suggested categories are: long service, helpfulness, cheerfulness, best behaved, well dressed, etc. As each category and winner is read out, that person comes out and receives a certificate. (Give each chosen leader a bag of sweets as well. These should be shared with their group at Bible time, although the children do not know this at this point.) Once they have been applauded they return to their seats. The people chosen to receive the awards do not necessarily fulfil the criteria, e.g. the person receiving the long service award could be a relatively new member of the group. After the chosen people have resumed their seats ask the children if what you did was fair? Why not?

In today's true story from the Bible we will learn about something that was for everyone, not just a few. Come back and tell me what it was.

Bible Time

At the beginning of the session refer back to Acts 1:8. Where has the gospel spread so far?

10:1	Caesarea is a major port on the Mediterranean Sea. It was built by Herod the Great and was the place where the Roman governor had his principal residence. It is situated about thirty-two miles north of Joppa.
10:2	God-fearers were those Gentiles who subscribed to the Jewish faith but did not become proselytes and were not circumcised.
10:4	Memorial offering - see Leviticus 2:2-3.
10:6	A tanner dealt with dead animals, so would have been shunned by orthodox Jews.

10:12-14	See Leviticus 11:1-47 for the Jewish food laws.
10:23	Peter took 6 people with him (Acts 11:12).
10:30	'Four days ago'. On day one Cornelius received his vision. On day two Peter received his vision and Cornelius' messengers arrived. On day three Peter set out for Caesarea, and on day four Peter arrived at Caesarea.
10:34	God shows no favouritism - see also Deuteronomy 10:17, Romans 2:11, Ephesians 6:9. This was an amazing thought for Peter, who had been brought up to believe that all non-Jews were to be despised. The children need to be reminded that God is the same today and accepts anyone who comes to him through faith in Jesus Christ. The teacher needs to have examples of the type of person the children would find unacceptable.
10:38	Refers to Jesus' baptism.
10:41	Emphasises the fact of Jesus' bodily resurrection.
10:42	The Jesus who is Saviour is the Jesus who will judge the living and the dead.
10:43	See Isaiah 53.
10:46	See Acts 11:15 - the speaking in other tongues was the same as the disciples did at Pentecost.

Synopsis

A devout Gentile named Cornelius is instructed by an angel to send men to find the apostle Peter and bring him back to Cornelius. As the men approach Joppa, where Peter is staying, Peter has a vision from God in which certain 'unclean' foods are laid before Peter. God declares the food to be clean and instructs Peter to not call anything unclean that God has declared to be clean. God also instructs Peter to go with the men who are looking for him. Just then these men arrive and Peter goes with them to Cornelius' house where a crowd has gathered. Peter tells them the good news about Jesus and while he is speaking the Holy Spirit comes on those who hear and they begin speaking in different languages as the apostles had done on the day of Pentecost. The Jews who were with Peter saw what happened and knew that these people had really received the gift of the Holy Spirit. Peter instructs them to baptise these new Christians.

Visual aids

Pictures or flannelgraph. You need Peter, Cornelius, an angel, messengers (optional) and a sheet containing animals, birds and reptiles. Visual aids can be found on pages 85-93.

A map is useful to show where Peter has been (see page 15).

Fun Sheets

5-7s   Photocopy pages 46 and 47 back to back for each child.

8-11s   Photocopy pages 48 and 49 back to back for each child.

Consolidation

Game 1: Prepare six cards with different statements about the group, one statement per card. Suggested statements are: anyone with brown shoes, anyone with blond hair, anyone with white socks, anyone with blue eyes, anyone with black shoes, anyone who is over 5ft. 6ins. tall. Make sure that the six statements collectively include the entire group so that no-one will be left out.

The children and leaders form a large circle holding hands. The circle moves round in a clockwise direction until the command is given to freeze. This could be done to music, stopping the music to stop the circle, or by calling out, 'Gentiles!' One of the children chooses an envelope containing one of the six cards and reads out the statement. All those who qualify form a smaller circle within the larger circle. Repeat, with the two circles moving in opposite directions, until all six statements have been read out. By the end everyone should have transferred from the outside circle to the inside circle. When the inside circle becomes bigger than the outside circle the people in the outside circle stop holding hands.

Game 2: A game of 'local' musical statues! Many paper plates/pieces of paper are scattered around the play area. Each paper plate has the name of a local city, town or suburb known to the children written on it. The children are 'The Good News' and can be labelled as such. When the music plays, the children run around the 'world'. When the music stops, they run to stand on a paper plate. Paper plates can be removed as the game continues in order to eliminate players. If you have many players, take out a few plates at a time. If playing this game indoors on a smooth surface, make sure the children won't slip on the paper and fall. It would be good to have the younger children playing the game first and the older group thereafter.

Wind Up

Remind the children about the warm-up and go over the answer to the question. The good news about Jesus is not just for a few people, but for everyone. How does God choose people? Does he choose people in the way they were chosen in Game 1? God's salvation is not just for some people who live in certain countries or who have a certain skin colour. God wants all people to be made right with him and join his family. God has chosen to use us to take the good news to people not only in our neighbourhood, our suburb, our city, our country, but also to our neighbouring countries and to countries far away as illustrated by Game 2.

Gentile Believers

Acts 10:1-48

Cornelius was a centurion in the Italian Regiment. See if you can find these pictures on the soldier. They tell us what kind of man Cornelius was.

- Loved God ♡

- Gave to the poor

- Prayed

- Saw an angel

Draw what Peter saw in his vision

Peter went to Cornelius' house to teach his household about Jesus. They believed the good news and got the same gift as the apostles. What was the gift?

Holy Spirit

Draw a line to connect the square to the shapes that have the correct answers and discover an important lesson that Peter and his friends learned about the message of Jesus.

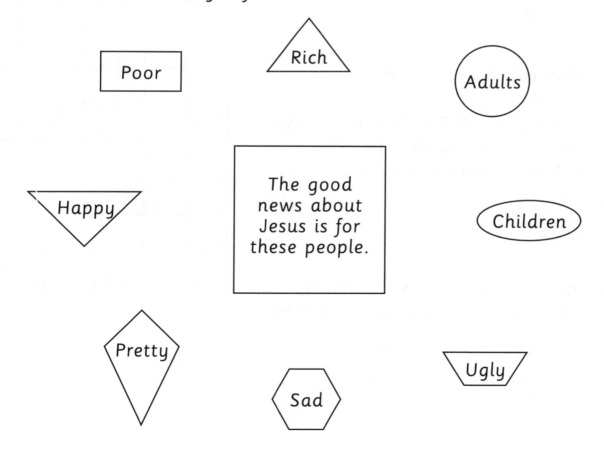

Poor

Rich

Adults

Happy

The good news about Jesus is for these people.

Children

Pretty

Sad

Ugly

Gentile Believers

Acts 10:1-48

Do you think there is anyone who does not need to hear the message about Jesus? Why / why not?

ACROSS

3. Cornelius sent three men here.
6. The name of the centurion.
8. Cornelius did this regularly.
9. Cornelius saw this.

DOWN

1. Cornelius gave money to them.
2. Simon's job.
4. Cornelius saw this at 3 o' clock in the afternoon.
5. The type of soldier that Cornelius was.
7. Simon Peter was staying near here.

Draw three of the animals that Peter might have seen in his vision. Leviticus 11:1-47 may give you some clues.

What did Peter think the vision meant? (Acts 10:14)

What did the vision actually mean? (Acts 10:19-20, 34-35)

Unscramble the words and write them in the spaces. Write down the circled letters from left to right and top to bottom in the spaces below to discover Peter's friends' reaction.

1. T S C A ◯ C _ ◯

2. F I T G G _ _ ◯

3. O Y L H _ ◯ _ Y

4. I N I A P G S R P R _ _ S _ ◯ _

5. S V L R B I E E E B _ L ◯ _ V E _ ◯

6. E D A H R ◯ ◯ _ A R ◯

Peter's friends were ___ ___ ___ ___ ___ ___ ___ ___ ___ ___ ___ ___ ___ ___ ___

Peter and his friends at first didn't believe that the good news about Jesus was also for those who were not Jews. Why does everyone need to hear about Jesus?

Think about someone you wouldn't normally speak to about Jesus. Has this lesson changed your mind?

Start-up Activities

The following are suggestions to use with the children as they arrive at the club. They are based on the book of Acts and each should take not more than ten minutes.

1. **Visitor's Passports:** The children draw themselves on the face outline.

2. **Play Dough Relief Map:** Using a large thick piece of cardboard for a base and play dough for the construction material (blue for the sea and brown for the land) the children make a relief map of Palestine together. As this activity can be worked on for more than one session, various items may be gradually added to the map e.g. town names (labelled toothpicks), boats on water, little houses (matchboxes) etc.

   Play Dough Recipe:

   Ingredients
   - 500ml flour
   - 500ml cold water
   - 30ml oil
   - 200ml salt
   - 30ml cream of tartar
   - Food colouring

   Method
   - Mix all the ingredients together.
   - Only after the ingredients are well mixed should they be placed on a medium heat stove and stirred continuously. Cook until it forms a ball (it will get lumpy first – just keep stirring!).
   - Place the dough on a working surface to cool.
   - When cool, knead until it has a nice soft, non-tacky consistency.
   - Store in a plastic bag, removing as much of the air as possible.

3. **Gospel Beads:** The children thread coloured beads onto lengths of shearing elastic in a particular order and tie the ends together to form a bracelet. They can use bracelets to tell their friends and family about Jesus. The order of beads should be as follows: Grey (sin that separates us from God); red (Jesus' death on the cross - He was punished in our place); white (when we trust in Jesus, our sin is washed away); green (growth as Christians); yellow/ gold (representing the golden streets of heaven where those who have trusted Jesus will never be separated from God again).

4. **Skittles:** To make the skittles, fill a number of empty plastic bottles with a bit of sand to weigh them down slightly. Cover the bottles using a neutral colour paper and glue. Draw faces and clothes on these 'Christians'. Write the names of apostles on a few of the bottles. Place the men on a circle of coloured paper (this is Jerusalem). Using a medium sized ball, roll it at the skittles, trying to miss the apostles. This is a picture of the Christians being scattered during the persecution. All were scattered except the apostles. You may want to put a bit more sand in the 'apostles' and no sand at all in the other 'Christians' if playing indoors to make them scatter further.

5. **Chariot Beetle:** Each team (minimum two players per team) needs a piece of paper, a pen and a die. They will draw a chariot in parts. The part drawn is decided by the roll of the die.
   - 6 is for the body of the chariot of which there is 1.
   - 5 is for the wheels of which there are 2.
   - 4 is for the horse of which there are 2.
   - 3 is for the Ethiopian of which there is 1.
   - 2 is for Philip of which there is 1.
   - 1 is for the scroll of which there is 1.

   A 6 must be rolled before any other chariot pieces may be added. The first team to draw all the required parts is the winner.

6. **Kim's Game:** Collect pictures or toys of the creatures of Acts 10:12 (c.f. Lev 11) – not more than ten for the first few games. Place them on a large sheet. As the game begins, open the sheet on the floor. After thirty seconds, gather the corners of the sheet and remove it. Each child must make a list on a piece of paper of all the creatures that can be remembered. The one who remembers the most is the winner. This game can be played in teams. You may want to get leaders/children to help with laying out the sheet and gathering it up again.

Lesson 1 - The Great Commission

- Print the activity onto white card; cutting out one item per child.
- They simply fold along the dashed line with text facing outwards then glue the edge that stretches from the apex to the base, thus leaving the base of the triangle open.
- When they insert a drinking straw into the pocket and blow; the triangle flies into the air and comes down again. (Jesus ascended into heaven and will return again in the same way).

Lesson 2 - Beginning in Jerusalem

- Print the activity onto white card.
- Cut along the solid lines. Each child requires one cut out and a paper clip.
- Colour to decorate.
- Fold the 'blades' in opposite directions on the dashed line so that it resembles helicopter blades.
- Place a paperclip over the x to provide additional weight.
- Throw it in the air and watch the 'tongues of fire' come spinning down to earth!

Jesus sent the Holy Spirit as promised (Acts 2:33).

Jesus sent the Holy Spirit as promised (Acts 2:33).

Jesus sent the Holy Spirit as promised (Acts 2:33).

Jesus sent the Holy Spirit as promised (Acts 2:33).

Jesus sent the Holy Spirit as promised (Acts 2:33).

Jesus sent the Holy Spirit as promised (Acts 2:33).

Lesson 3 - Opposition

Activity for 5-7s

- Print the activity onto white card and cut along the solid lines for each child.
- The children will do the following:
  - Use sticky tape to paste cut drinking straws on the opening representing prison bars. Mould two small pieces of aluminium foil to make two swords and paste them either side of the prison bars on the opposite side to represent the soldiers guarding the prison.
  - On the bottom half of the page draw a few apostles who are speaking the words "Believe in the Lord Jesus and you will be saved".

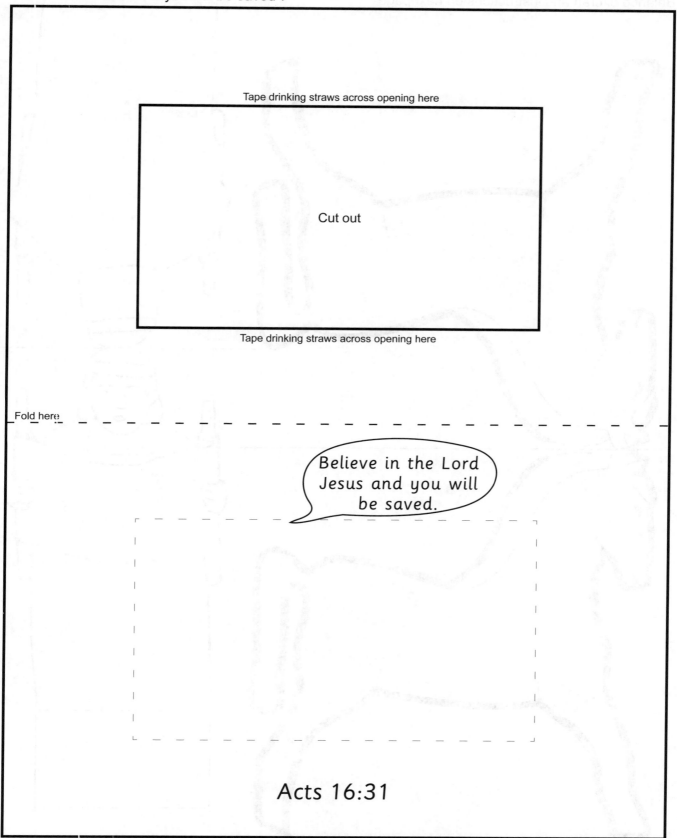

Tape drinking straws across opening here

Cut out

Tape drinking straws across opening here

Fold here

Believe in the Lord Jesus and you will be saved.

Acts 16:31

Lesson 4 - Persecution

- Pre-prepare white pieces of paper with the memory verse written on it using a white wax crayon.
- The children are to sponge water paint over the paper revealing the memory verse.
- Be sure to use adequate protection for clothing and have warm soapy water handy for hand washing.

Lesson 5 - Into Samaria

Balance of craft and instructions on next page.

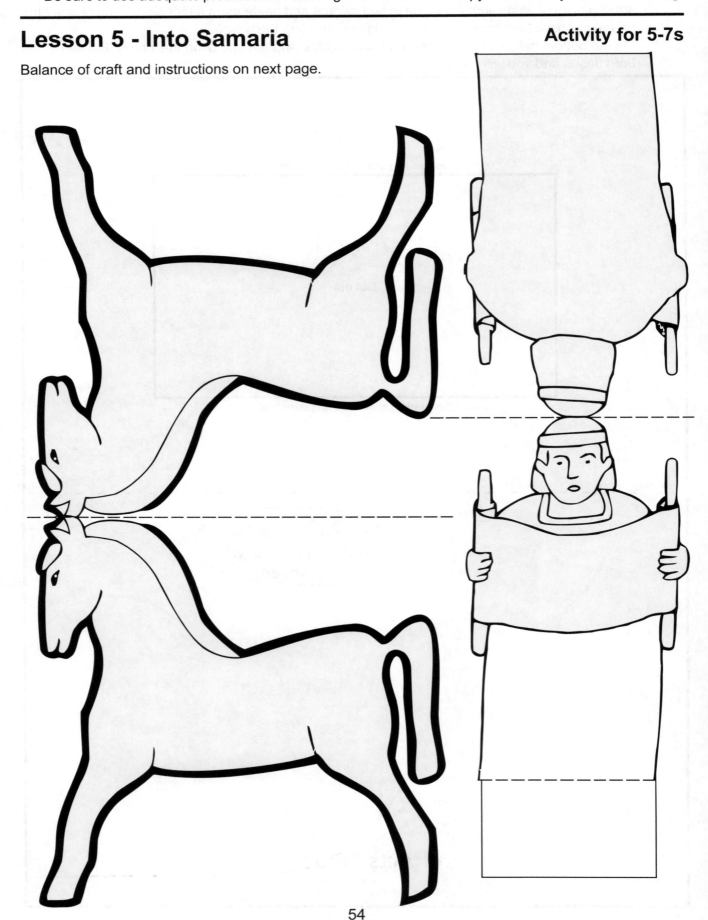

Each child requires both pages photocopied on card, one drinking straw cut to 15 cms, one garden stick cut to 9 cms and two wheels cut from a bottle cork.

1. Bend and glue one chariot base on top of the other one. Decorate the body of the chariot.
2. Colour the Ethiopian, fold in half and glue. Bend the tab back and glue to the base of the chariot in front of the marks for the wheels.
3. Make holes at X on both sides and the front of the chariot. Insert the garden stick through the side holes. Thread a cork wheel followed by a card wheel onto both ends. Secure the ends of the stick with a blob of blu-tack.
4. Colour the horse and fold in half. Sellotape one end of the drinking straw inside one of the horse's sides with the long end protruding from the back. Glue the two head and tail sections together to provide rigidity. Insert the back of the straw through the hole on the front of the chariot.

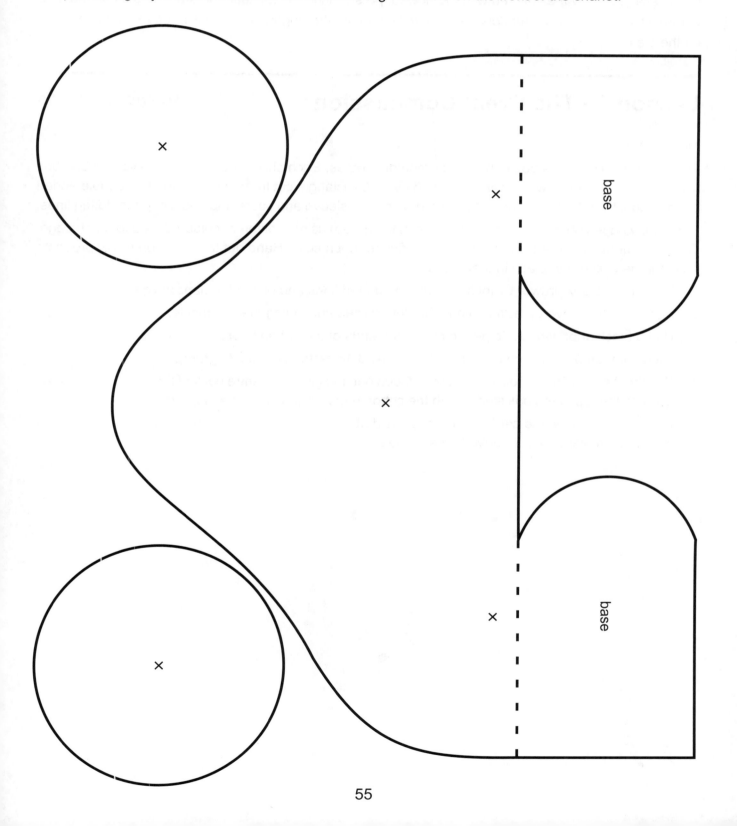

Lesson 6 - Gentile Believers

Each child needs a paper plate and a piece of cloth about the same size as the plate. Each child is given a portion of air-drying clay. They will use it to make animals which they should place on the plate to dry. Supply the children with items such as toothpicks to add detail to their creations. Give some guidance in terms of the kinds of animals that were on the sheet - see Leviticus 11:1-47.

Alternately, one could use papier-mâché to make the animals. For the glue simply mix together one part flour to two parts water. Mix well to remove any lumps. If you live in an area of high humidity, add a little bit of salt to prevent mould. This glue can be stored in a covered container in the fridge for a few days if necessary. Supply the children with old newspapers which they will tear into strips and dip in the glue to make their models. The models take a few days to dry thoroughly and so will need to be taken home on the plate.

Lesson 1 - The Great Commission

Memory Verse Box

The children will make a box to hold their memory verses. Each child requires one sleeve and one box from page 57 photocopied on card, a 2 Timothy 3:16 rectangle cut from page 58 and two double ended cotton buds. Prior to the lesson cut out the drawer and sleeve and score and fold along the dotted lines.

Photocopy pages 59-63 (once per 8 children in the group) using a different coloured card for each page. Cut out a memory verse card for days two to five for each child. Hand out the cards on the appropriate days for the children to place in their boxes.

1. Make up the box drawer by folding along the dotted lines and gluing the flaps inside.
2. Make up the sleeve by folding along the dotted lines and gluing the flap inside.
3. Use a black or brown felt tip pen to colour the ends of the cotton buds.
4. Glue a cotton bud to each end of the 2 Timothy 3:16 rectangle (see diagram).
5. Roll the 2 ends of the scroll to the centre. Open out and glue the centre back of the scroll to the top of the box sleeve with the cotton buds lengthways (see diagram).
6. Fold the memory verse card in half along the dotted line and place in the drawer. Slide the drawer into the sleeve to make the box.

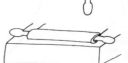

Sleeve

Sleeve

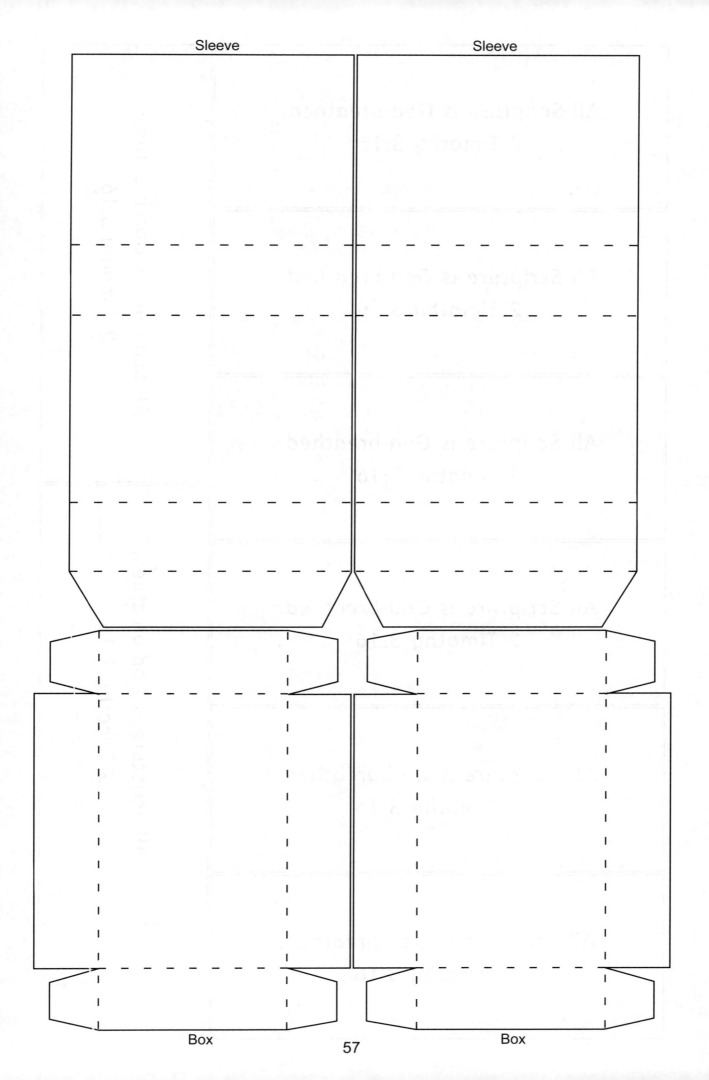

Box

57

Box

All Scripture is God-breathed.
2 Timothy 3:16

All Scripture is God-breathed.
2 Timothy 3:16

All Scripture is God-breathed.
2 Timothy 3:16

All Scripture is God-breathed.
2 Timothy 3:16

All Scripture is God-breathed.
2 Timothy 3:16

All Scripture is God-breathed.
2 Timothy 3:16

All Scripture is God-breathed.
2 Timothy 3:16

All Scripture is God-breathed.
2 Timothy 3:16

You will be my witnesses
in Jerusalem, and in all
Judea and Samaria, and
to the ends of the earth.
Acts 1:8

You will be my witnesses
in Jerusalem, and in all
Judea and Samaria, and
to the ends of the earth.
Acts 1:8

You will be my witnesses
in Jerusalem, and in all
Judea and Samaria, and
to the ends of the earth.
Acts 1:8

You will be my witnesses
in Jerusalem, and in all
Judea and Samaria, and
to the ends of the earth.
Acts 1:8

You will be my witnesses
in Jerusalem, and in all
Judea and Samaria, and
to the ends of the earth.
Acts 1:8

You will be my witnesses
in Jerusalem, and in all
Judea and Samaria, and
to the ends of the earth.
Acts 1:8

You will be my witnesses
in Jerusalem, and in all
Judea and Samaria, and
to the ends of the earth.
Acts 1:8

You will be my witnesses
in Jerusalem, and in all
Judea and Samaria, and
to the ends of the earth.
Acts 1:8

Christ died for sins once for
all, to bring you to God.
1 Peter 3:18

Christ died for sins once for
all, to bring you to God.
1 Peter 3:18

Christ died for sins once for
all, to bring you to God.
1 Peter 3:18

Christ died for sins once for
all, to bring you to God.
1 Peter 3:18

Christ died for sins once for
all, to bring you to God.
1 Peter 3:18

Christ died for sins once for
all, to bring you to God.
1 Peter 3:18

Christ died for sins once for
all, to bring you to God.
1 Peter 3:18

Christ died for sins once for
all, to bring you to God.
1 Peter 3:18

Believe in the Lord Jesus,
and you will be saved.
Acts 16:31

Believe in the Lord Jesus,
and you will be saved.
Acts 16:31

Believe in the Lord Jesus,
and you will be saved.
Acts 16:31

Believe in the Lord Jesus,
and you will be saved.
Acts 16:31

Believe in the Lord Jesus,
and you will be saved.
Acts 16:31

Believe in the Lord Jesus,
and you will be saved.
Acts 16:31

Believe in the Lord Jesus,
and you will be saved.
Acts 16:31

Believe in the Lord Jesus,
and you will be saved.
Acts 16:31

I am not ashamed of the gospel, because it is the power of God for the salvation of everyone who believes.

Romans 1:16

I am not ashamed of the gospel, because it is the power of God for the salvation of everyone who believes.

Romans 1:16

I am not ashamed of the gospel, because it is the power of God for the salvation of everyone who believes.

Romans 1:16

I am not ashamed of the gospel, because it is the power of God for the salvation of everyone who believes.

Romans 1:16

I am not ashamed of the gospel, because it is the power of God for the salvation of everyone who believes.

Romans 1:16

I am not ashamed of the gospel, because it is the power of God for the salvation of everyone who believes.

Romans 1:16

I am not ashamed of the gospel, because it is the power of God for the salvation of everyone who believes.

Romans 1:16

I am not ashamed of the gospel, because it is the power of God for the salvation of everyone who believes.

Romans 1:16

God commands all people
everywhere to repent.
Acts 17:30

God commands all people
everywhere to repent.
Acts 17:30

God commands all people
everywhere to repent.
Acts 17:30

God commands all people
everywhere to repent.
Acts 17:30

God commands all people
everywhere to repent.
Acts 17:30

God commands all people
everywhere to repent.
Acts 17:30

God commands all people
everywhere to repent.
Acts 17:30

God commands all people
everywhere to repent.
Acts 17:30

Lesson 2 - Beginning in Jerusalem

- Print the activity onto white card.
- Cut along the solid lines. Each child requires one cut out and a paper clip.
- Colour to decorate.
- Fold the 'blades' in opposite directions on the dashed line so that it resembles helicopter blades.
- Place a paperclip over the x to provide additional weight.
- Throw it in the air and watch the 'tongues of fire' come spinning down to earth!

Jesus sent the Holy Spirit as promised (Acts 2:33).

Jesus sent the Holy Spirit as promised (Acts 2:33).

Jesus sent the Holy Spirit as promised (Acts 2:33).

Jesus sent the Holy Spirit as promised (Acts 2:33).

Jesus sent the Holy Spirit as promised (Acts 2:33).

Jesus sent the Holy Spirit as promised (Acts 2:33).

Lesson 3 - Opposition

Activity for 8-11s

Print the activity on to white card and cut out along the solid lines (UK / European covers on next page). Each child needs one light switch cover which they can decorate with potato stamps and poster paint or jewels or simply stickers (ensure there are some really fun stickers for girls and boys). Encourage the children to pray every night when they switch off the light for Christians all over the world who are being opposed for telling people to believe in Jesus.

Believe in the Lord Jesus

cut out

and you will be saved.

Acts 16:31

Believe in the Lord Jesus

cut out

and you will be saved.

Acts 16:31

Believe in the Lord Jesus

cut out

and you will be saved.

Acts 16:31

Believe in the Lord Jesus

cut out

and you will be saved.

Acts 16:31

UK / European light switch covers.

Believe in the Lord Jesus

cut out

and you will be saved.

Acts 16:31

Believe in the Lord Jesus

cut out

and you will be saved.

Acts 16:31

Believe in the Lord Jesus

cut out

and you will be saved.

Acts 16:31

Believe in the Lord Jesus

cut out

and you will be saved.

Acts 16:31

Believe in the Lord Jesus

cut out

and you will be saved.

Acts 16:31

Believe in the Lord Jesus

cut out

and you will be saved.

Acts 16:31

Lesson 4 - Persecution

Activity for 8-11s

Gospel Feet Sun Catcher

Requirements:

- Hole Punch
- Glue stick
- Tissue Paper
- Photocopy acetate film
- Scissors
- Wool or string

Instructions:

Copy the foot pattern on page 68 onto acetate film and cut out. Each child gets one foot to decorate. They do this by gluing various bits of torn tissue paper onto the pattern. Trim the edges if necessary and punch the hole as marked. Use wool or string to hang the sun catcher in front of a window.

Lesson 5 - Into Samaria

Activity for 8-11s

Talking People

Photocopy page 69 onto card (there are enough items for two children per page). Cut out the heads and two strips and make holes at x. The children colour the heads and attach the strips to the heads with split pin paper fasteners (see diagram). Peter can be made to talk to the other head by pushing and pulling on the two side strips. The listener nods in agreement.

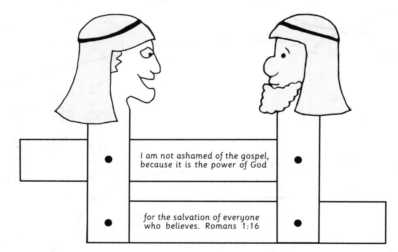

I am not ashamed of the gospel, because it is the power of God

for the salvation of everyone who believes. Romans 1:16

Lesson 6 - Gentile Believers

Activity for 8-11s

Each child needs a paper plate and a piece of cloth about the same size as the plate. Each child is given a portion of air-drying clay. They will use it to make animals which they should place on the plate to dry. Supply the children with items such as toothpicks to add detail to their creations. Give some guidance in terms of the kinds of animals that were on the sheet - see Leviticus 11:1-47.

Alternately, one could use papier-mâché to make the animals. For the glue simply mix together one part flour to two parts water. Mix well to remove any lumps. If you live in an area of high humidity, add a little bit of salt to prevent mould. This glue can be stored in a covered container in the fridge for a few days if necessary. Supply the children with old newspapers which they will tear into strips and dip in the glue to make their models. There models take a few days to dry thoroughly and so will need to be taken home on the plate.

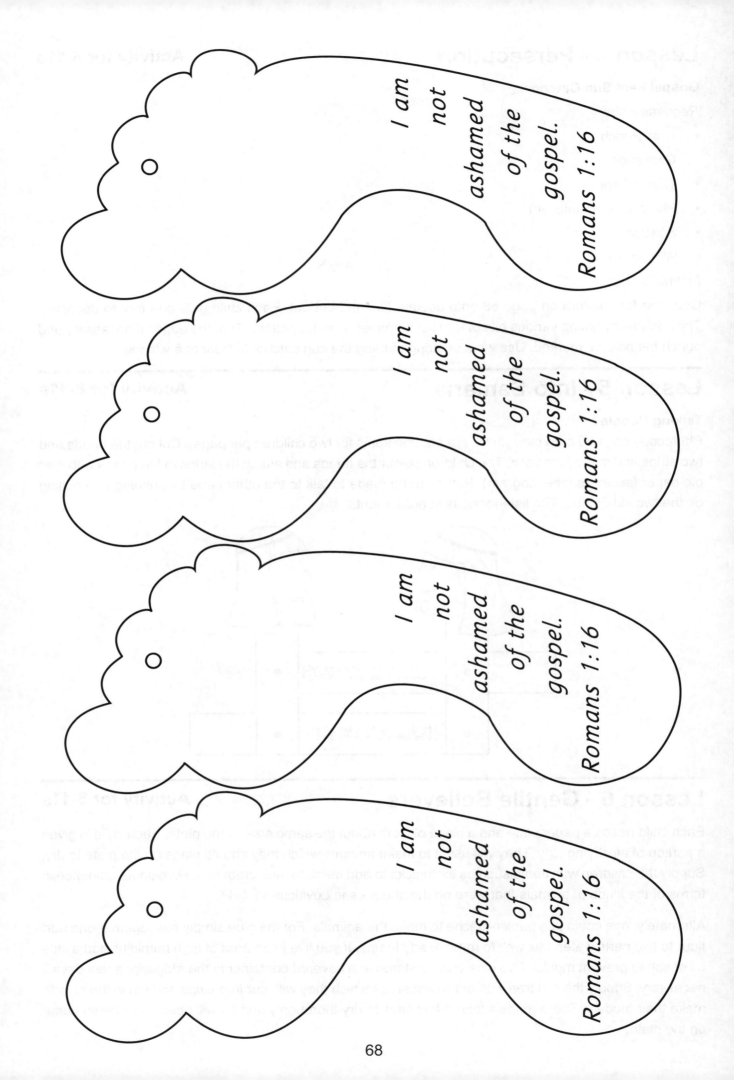

I am
not
ashamed
of the
gospel.
Romans 1:16

I am
not
ashamed
of the
gospel.
Romans 1:16

I am
not
ashamed
of the
gospel.
Romans 1:16

I am
not
ashamed
of the
gospel.
Romans 1:16

for the salvation of everyone
who believes. Romans 1:16

I am not ashamed of the gospel,
because it is the power of God

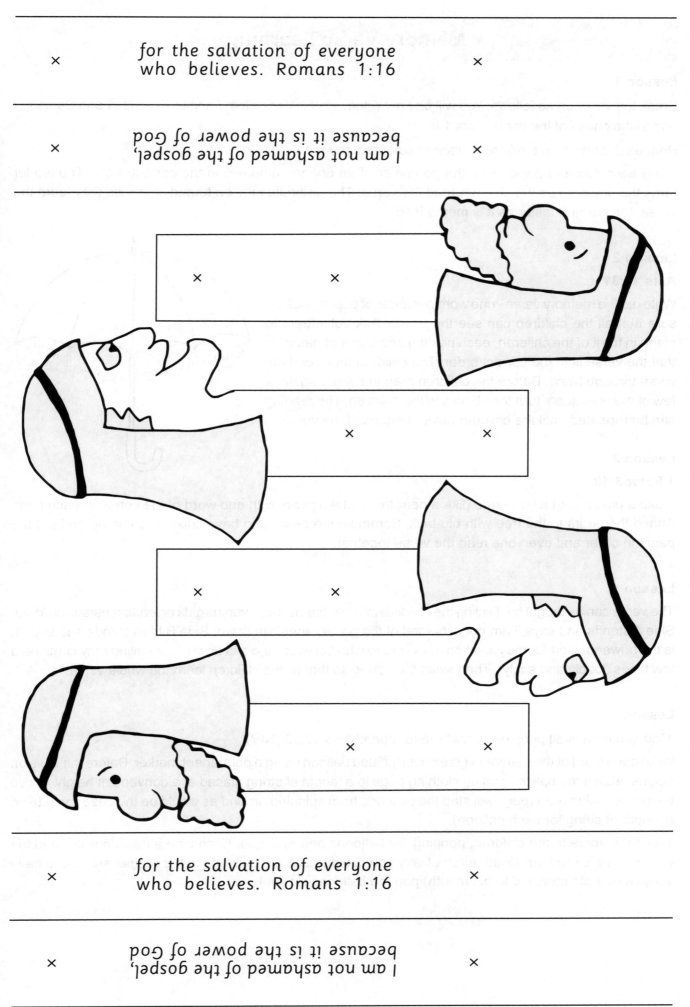

for the salvation of everyone
who believes. Romans 1:16

I am not ashamed of the gospel,
because it is the power of God

69

Memory Verse Learning

Lesson 1

Break the verse up as follows: You will be / my witnesses / in Jerusalem / and in all Judea / and Samaria / and to the ends / of the earth / Acts 1:8.

Print each portion on a different piece of coloured paper.

Hang each piece of paper from the perimeter of an opened umbrella in the correct order. The leader turns the umbrella as the children read the verse. The umbrella may be turned slowly as they learn the verse, then turned faster as it is memorised.

Lesson 2

Acts 16:31

Write out the memory verse - one word per sheet of paper - making sure that all the children can see the words. Ask volunteers to stand in front of the children, each holding one sheet of paper so that the verse is in the correct order. The children then read the verse through twice. Before the children read the verse again, a few of the volunteers turn their backs to the children. The reading can be repeated until the children have memorised the verse.

Lesson 3

1 Peter 3:18

Make a poster with a large tree (like a pear tree). Make pears with one word of the verse on each pear. Attach the pears to the tree with blu-tack. Scramble the pears and have children come up and put the pears in order and everyone read the verse together.

Lesson 4

The verse can be taught by dividing the children into two teams; boys versus girls or leaders versus children. Side A stands and says 'I am not ashamed of the gospel' then sits down. Side B then stands and says 'It is the power of God for the salvation of everyone who believes' and sits down. The calling may continue a few times (loudly and softly). Then swap the calling so that all the children learn the whole verse.

Lesson 5

'God commands all people everywhere to repent' Acts 17:30 (NIV).

Write each word of the memory verse on an inflated balloon using a permanent marker. Before the session begins, attach the balloons using clothing pegs to a length of string placed at a convenient height above the presentation area (pegs will stop the balloons from spinning around as would be the case if you used a length of string for each balloon).

Teach the verse to the children, popping the balloons one at a time. Each time a balloon is popped the entire verse is read out aloud. Alternatively you could attach the balloons to the puppet stand and have Toby (with a pin attached to his mouth) pop the balloons for you!

Quizzes

A quiz is a useful way of testing how much has been learnt from the Bible story. The questions should be related to the Bible passage and appropriate to the age and understanding of the children. There needs to be an element of chance built in to prevent too much competition causing distress to children who get the answer wrong. This is done by each team attempting to complete some task, e.g. collecting six scrolls. Each team requires a set of eight identical shapes numbered on the back randomly from one to eight. Two of the set are marked on the front in some way to distinguish them from the remaining six. Pin the shapes onto a board with the numbered side uppermost.

The group is split into two teams of equal intellectual ability. Questions are asked of each team alternately. If a child answers a question correctly he/she is allowed to choose one of the numbered pieces from the board. The chosen piece is turned over and, if it is one of the six to be collected, is pinned onto the board. If the chosen piece is one of the two 'bad' shapes it is placed to one side. If a wrong answer is given the question is passed to the other side.

A quiz should last about 10 - 15 minutes. This will allow each side to collect six items out of eight. A minimum of sixteen questions needs to be prepared. Remember to include some questions suitable for the younger members of the team.

Lesson 1 - The Great Commission
Each team requires a set of eight clouds, six white and two grey.

Lesson 2 - Beginning in Jerusalem
Each team requires a set of eight tongues of fire, six coloured in red and orange and two coloured grey.

Lesson 3 - Opposition
Each team requires a set of eight megaphones, six with sound coming out and two that have been 'silenced'.

Lesson 4 - Persecution
Each team requires a set of eight faces, six with smiles (those who accept the gospel) and two looking angry (those who reject the gospel).

Lesson 5 - Into Samaria
Each team requires a set of eight scrolls, six with legible text on and two with illegible scribble (see diagram).

Lesson 6 - Gentile Believers
Each team requires a set of eight pigs, six coloured pink and two plain white.

All these images can be found on page 78 - enlarge as required.

A Day in the Life of Toby and Trudy - Keeping Promises

Trudy Hi Toby. Guess what?

Toby What?

Trudy Today, I'm going to tell a most astonishing story.

Toby Is it the story about the little girl?

Trudy Yes, it has a little girl in it.

Toby And three bears?

Trudy No, it's not Goldilocks and the Three Bears.

Toby I want to hear Goldilocks and the Three Bears.

Trudy This story is not about Goldilocks and the Three Bears.

Toby I want to hear about the porridge. I love porridge. Especially when it's just right.

Trudy Toby, I told you this is not Goldilocks. Now, once upon a time, a long, long…

Toby I want broken chairs and messed up beds.

Trudy Toby, I'm trying to tell this most astonishing story, and you keep interrupting. That's rude and it's not fair to the other boys and girls, who want to hear this story.

Toby Sorreeee! But I want to hear about Baby Bear whining.

Trudy But I'm not ready to tell that story today.

Toby Can't you do it from memory?

Trudy Probably, but that's not what I promised to do.

Toby So what? People break promises to me all the time.

Trudy What does that have to do with this story?

Toby Well, if people break promises to me, then you can break promises to them.

Trudy No, I don't think it works that way.

Toby What do you mean?

Trudy Well, if I promised to do one thing and did something else instead, soon no one would trust me.

Toby They wouldn't?

Trudy No. How do you feel when people make a promise to you and then break it?

Toby First, I feel bad. It makes me feel like I did something wrong. Then I get mad.

Trudy See. That's exactly how others feel when you break promises to them.

Toby They do? Oh! [*thoughtfully*]

Trudy   You know Jesus never broke any of his promises?

Toby   Really? Not even a single one?

Trudy   Not even a single one.

Toby   Wow, that's amazing.

Trudy   Yes, come along I'll tell you all about it.

[Exit both puppets]

Leader - Well, hopefully Toby has now learnt that you can't just go around breaking your promises.

In today's true story from the Bible we will see what happened when someone made a promise. Come back and tell me:

1. Who made the promise?

2. What was promised?

3. Where did the promise-maker go?

A Day in the Life of Toby and Trudy - Jealousy Makes You Nasty!

Trudy   [enters - humming to herself]

Toby   [enters] Hey, Trudy. You're in a good mood. What's up?

Trudy   Well, Sarah's mum gave me two tickets to go to the theme park this afternoon. Mum says we can go after lunch. Isn't that just too exciting for words? [sings the same tune as before, moving head from side to side, 'I am so happy, I am so happy' - in an almost taunting manner.]

Toby   Cool! I'll get my shoes on. I've always wanted to go to the theme park. Those rides look as if they are extremely fast. I hope I can get some cotton candy too. The white one, though. I'm sure it tastes better than the pink one. [To Trudy] Should I bring a coat? In case it gets cold later?

Trudy   Uhm. No. You're actually NOT going with me. Rachel is, though. And she is bringing her coat. Thanks.

Toby   [Indignant] What? Why is she going and not me? Is it because she is a stinky girl?

Trudy   Toby, she is going with me because she is my friend and she is tall enough! You know that you have to be the right height to go on those fast rides.

Toby   [sulking] Well, that's just not fair. You could take me but you're just being mean.

Trudy   No, I'm not!

Toby   Yes, you are!

Trudy   No, I'm not!

Toby   Yes, you are!

Trudy   Toby, that's just not true. I'm not being mean. You're my brother and I would love to go with you but we need to obey the rules of the theme park. You're just jealous.

Toby   Jealous? Me? Ha! You don't even know what that means.

Trudy   We can go to the theme park and you may not. It makes you feel angry. Then you say mean things like calling Rachel a 'stinky' girl.

Toby   [sulking] OK. So she's not stinky. [pause] I think the rules should change though. So what if I'm a bit shorter than you?

Trudy   You are a WHOLE LOT shorter than me. The rules are to keep us safe.

But what about this great idea…I'll buy some candy floss for you. I'm sure you could have it for dessert.

Toby   [brightens up] Would you really? Oh thanks, Trudy. You're the best sister ever.

Trudy   As soon as you are tall enough, I'm sure you will go to the theme park.

Toby   [both chat as they exit] Really?

Trudy   Yup. Maybe you will take me with you and then we…

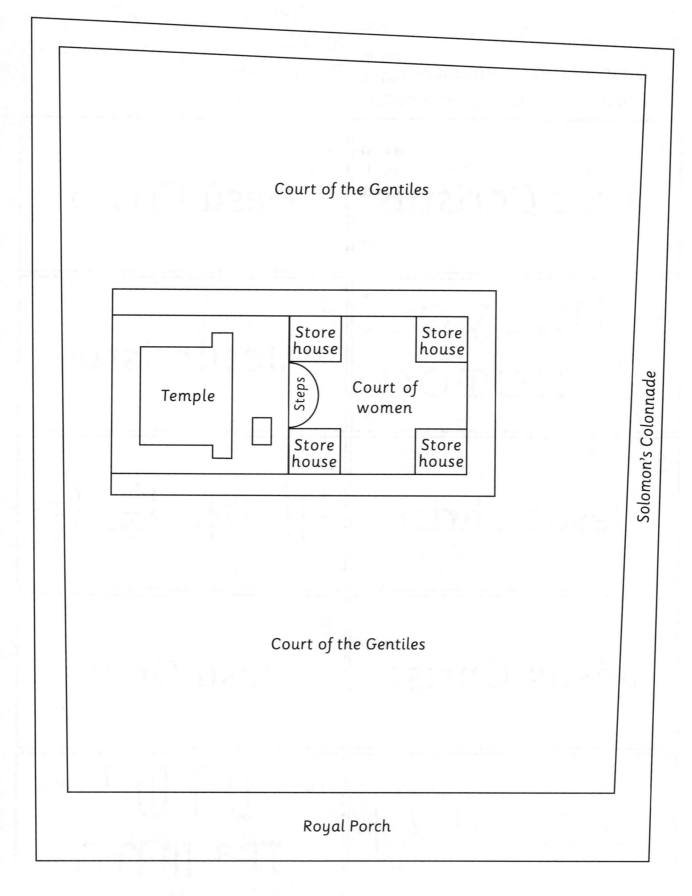

1. German
2. Italian
3. Russian
4. Spanish (South American)
5. English (UK, USA and others)
6. Chinese
7. French
8. Welsh
9. Japanese
10. Hebrew

1 **Jesus Christus**	2 **Gesù Cristo**
3 **Иисус Христос**	4 **Jesucristo**
5 **Jesus Christ**	6 **耶穌基督**
7 **Jésus-Christ**	8 **Iesu Grist**
9 **イエスキリスト**	10 **יֵשׁוּעַ הַמָּשִׁיחַ**

Task List

What Jesus said	You must find	To represent
1. That he would die	Two pieces of wood/twigs	The cross
2. That he would rise again	One stone	The stone that was rolled away
3. It was promised in the Old Testament	Something old	Old Testament
4. Turn back to God	A 'new leaf'	'turning over a new leaf' or repentance

Task List

What Jesus said	You must find	To represent
1. That he would die	Two pieces of wood/twigs	The cross
2. That he would rise again	One stone	The stone that was rolled away
3. It was promised in the Old Testament	Something old	Old Testament
4. Turn back to God	A 'new leaf'	'turning over a new leaf' or repentance

Task List

What Jesus said	You must find	To represent
1. That he would die	Two pieces of wood/twigs	The cross
2. That he would rise again	One stone	The stone that was rolled away
3. It was promised in the Old Testament	Something old	Old Testament
4. Turn back to God	A 'new leaf'	'turning over a new leaf' or repentance

Task List

What Jesus said	You must find	To represent
1. That he would die	Two pieces of wood/twigs	The cross
2. That he would rise again	One stone	The stone that was rolled away
3. It was promised in the Old Testament	Something old	Old Testament
4. Turn back to God	A 'new leaf'	'turning over a new leaf' or repentance

He was
led like a
sheep to the
slaughter

God's Good News

God made all things - even me.
Genesis 1:1,31

God loves me and wants me to be his friend.
John 3:16

But the wrong things I do put a barrier between me and God.
Isaiah 59:2

To take this barrier away, Jesus died on the cross.
Romans 5:8

Jesus rose from the dead to bring new life to all who believe in him.
Romans 4:25-5:1, 6:23

Sorry, God

If I want to be God's friend I must say sorry to God...
Acts 2:38

Jesus is my Saviour

I must believe that Jesus is God and that he can save me...
Acts 16:31

Jesus

and I must submit to Jesus as King of my life.
Philippians 2:10-11

Christ Jesus came into the world to save sinners.
1 Timothy 1:15

Bible Timeline

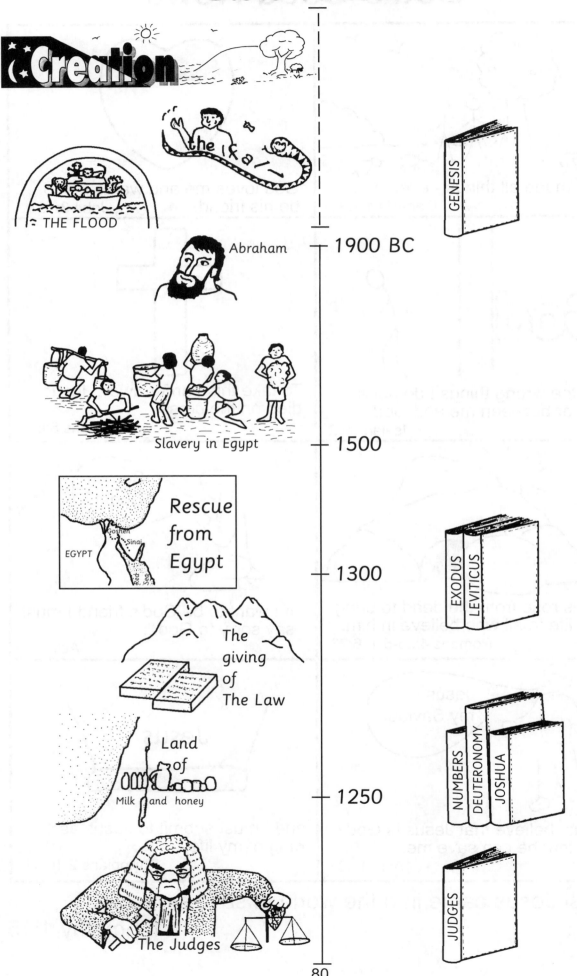

Creation

the Fall

THE FLOOD

Abraham

1900 BC

Slavery in Egypt

1500

Rescue from Egypt

EGYPT
Goshen
Sinai
Red Sea

1300

The giving of The Law

Land of Milk and honey

1250

The Judges

80

GENESIS

EXODUS
LEVITICUS

NUMBERS
DEUTERONOMY
JOSHUA

JUDGES

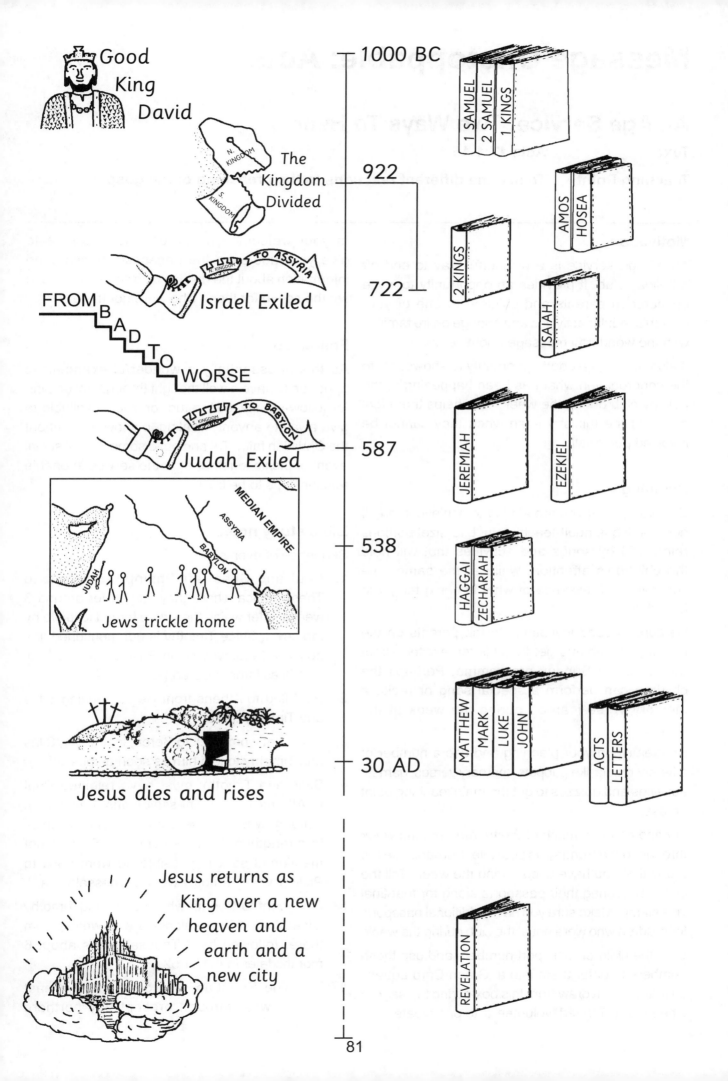

Good King David

The Kingdom Divided

FROM BAD TO WORSE

Israel Exiled

TO ASSYRIA

Judah Exiled

TO BABYLON

MEDIAN EMPIRE
ASSYRIA
BABYLON
JUDAH

Jews trickle home

Jesus dies and rises

Jesus returns as King over a new heaven and earth and a new city

1000 BC

922

722

587

538

30 AD

1 SAMUEL
2 SAMUEL
1 KINGS

2 KINGS

AMOS
HOSEA

ISAIAH

JEREMIAH
EZEKIEL

HAGGAI
ZECHARIAH

MATTHEW
MARK
LUKE
JOHN

ACTS
LETTERS

REVELATION

Message Unstoppable: Acts

All Age Service: Two Ways To Hear

Text   **Acts 17:1-15**

Teaching Point   **To see the different reactions to the preaching of the gospel.**

Motivation

An all age service is a wonderful way to end off a holiday club. It provides an opportunity to invite unchurched parents and children to one of your church's regular activities and engage entire families with the wonderful message about Jesus.

It also provides a good opportunity to showcase to the congregation what has been happening at the holiday club during the week. This helps them feel a part of the ministry even when they cannot be involved personally.

Planning

Generally, what you are aiming to achieve in an all age service is adult teaching in 'bite size' portions reinforced by songs and activities that will hold the children's attention, while at the same time conveying the essence of what is being taught to the adults.

Be sure to send invitations to the parents on the last day of club and get the children excited about attending the Sunday programme. Perhaps the children can perform a special song or recite a memory verse learned during the week at the service.

Be creative in your planning and use a number of different media like puppets, memory verses, games, activities and quizzes to get the main teaching point across.

Try and carry as much of the theme from the week through to the Sunday as possible. Perhaps use the props that you have used during the week. Tell the children to bring their passports along for that final visa stamp! Make sure you have additional passports for children who were not at the club during the week.

Give the children passport numbers and use those numbers to enter them into a 'Green Card Lottery' so that you can draw from this box during the service whenever you need 'volunteers' to participate.

In your welcome and introduction be sure to give your audience the necessary background information about the holiday club so that you have set the scene for those who were not there.

Follow-up

As this is essentially a wonderful evangelistic opportunity have a well thought through action plan for follow-up. Have literature or tracts available to give away to anyone wanting to know more about the Christian faith. Try and have some kind of social event or picnic together after the service to enable relationships to be built.

Bible study notes

Sequence of events

1. Paul and Silas left Philippi and went to Thessalonica where they stayed for around 3 weeks, after which they were forced to leave by the Jews. Since Timothy is not mentioned it is possible he stayed on in Philippi, joining Paul and Silas later in Berea (Acts 17:14).

2. Paul fled to Athens from Berea, leaving Silas and Timothy there.

3. Paul sent word back to Berea, instructing Silas and Timothy to join him as soon as possible.

4. Silas and Timothy must have rejoined Paul in Athens (see 1 Thessalonians 1:1; 3:1-2). Timothy was then sent back to Thessalonica to strengthen the new converts. Silas is not mentioned so it is possible he went back to Philippi when Timothy went to Thessalonica.

5. Paul went to Corinth where Silas and Timothy joined him. 1 Thessalonians was written from there, followed by 2 Thessalonians about 6 months later in AD 51/52.

17:1   The Egnatian Way crossed from east to west through present day northern

Greece and was a major trade route. Philippi, Amphipolis and Thessalonica were on this route and were, therefore, strategic centres. It was estimated that a person would travel 30 miles a day, so each city would be about that distance apart. Thessalonica, about 100 miles from Philippi, was a busy seaport and capital of the province of Macedonia.

17:2   As usual, Paul visited the synagogue first.

17:4   Prominent women could mean the wives of leading men, or women who deserved notice in their own right.

17:5   Jealousy motivated the Jews' reaction (cf. 13:45), because of the response of the Greeks and the women.

17:7   'Defying Caesar's decrees' - to support a rival to Caesar was treason for a Roman.

17:9   'On bail' - Jason would have to guarantee to keep the peace or else he could forfeit his property or even his life.

17:10   No mention of Timothy. Berea is modern day Veroia, about 50 miles from Thessalonica.

17:13   The Thessalonian Jews again orchestrated trouble for Paul and Silas.

17:15   Athens, with its university, was still a leading city in Paul's day. Five centuries earlier it had been at its height of glory in art, philosophy, etc.

Visual Aids

Have the leaders all wear 'super-sized' ears (see page 84).

Use a good map which clearly shows Amphipolis, Apollonia, Thesslonica and Berea (these are readily available on the internet). Highlight the different cities while the passage is being read.

Use life size, human-shaped cardboard cutouts to represent the jealous Thessalonian Jews and the Bereans. Print out the various attributes that describe these two groups of people and get the children to help you by fixing these attributes to the figures.

In this way you can build a very visual contrast between these two groups of people. They represent two responses to the same gospel message.

Focus Activity

Draw eight names from the 'Green Card Lottery' box and have the children stand in a line in front of the congregation. Whisper a funny sentence in the ear of the first child. Explain beforehand that you will only say it once and that this message needs to be transmitted down the line to the end. Get the last child to tell the congregation what the message was that they received. Ask the first child to say what they originally heard. Make the point that sometimes we do not always hear things properly and that we sometimes go on to act on the wrong information. Some people respond in the wrong way to the message about Jesus because they do not really understand the message.

Possible Points of Application

The contrast in this passage is between the response of the jealous Thessalonian Jews and everyone else who believed. This group of believers included prominent people, Gentiles and Jews. Paul was able to reason with them from the scriptures because the Christian gospel is reasonable and can be defended. The content of Paul's teaching is the death and resurrection of Jesus which proves that he is the Christ. The Bereans are commended because of their eager desire to discover the truth and their testing of Paul's message against the Old Testament scriptures - they were not simply gullible or ignorant.

Invite the people to be like the Bereans and investigate the truth about Jesus by reading one of the gospels. Maybe have some copies of Mark's gospel available for distribution.

Possible Programme Outline

Welcome, open in prayer and give background to holiday club.	5 mins
Song	5 mins
Focus activity	5 mins
Bible reading	5 mins
Song or puppet show	5 mins
Teaching slot - Thessalonians	10 mins
Children's song with actions	5 mins
Teaching slot - Bereans	10 mins
Challenge and closing song	5 mins

- Copy onto brightly coloured card.
- Cut out the ears and the two strips which form the headband.
- Join the two strips end to end and include the tab of each ear at the same time so that the writing will appear right way up on the forehead.
- Size by pinching the excess band material together and fold over. Use sticky tape or a staple to secure.

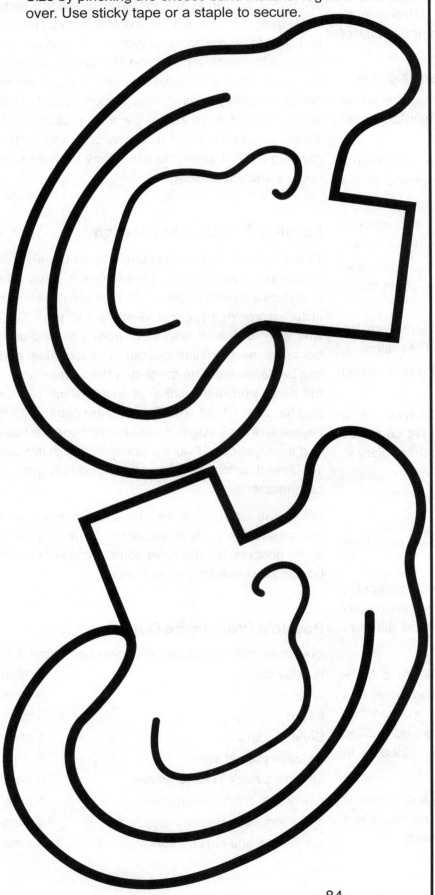

Angel

Centurion

Stephen

Angry men

Baptism

Apostles

Foreigners

Chariot

Critical Jews

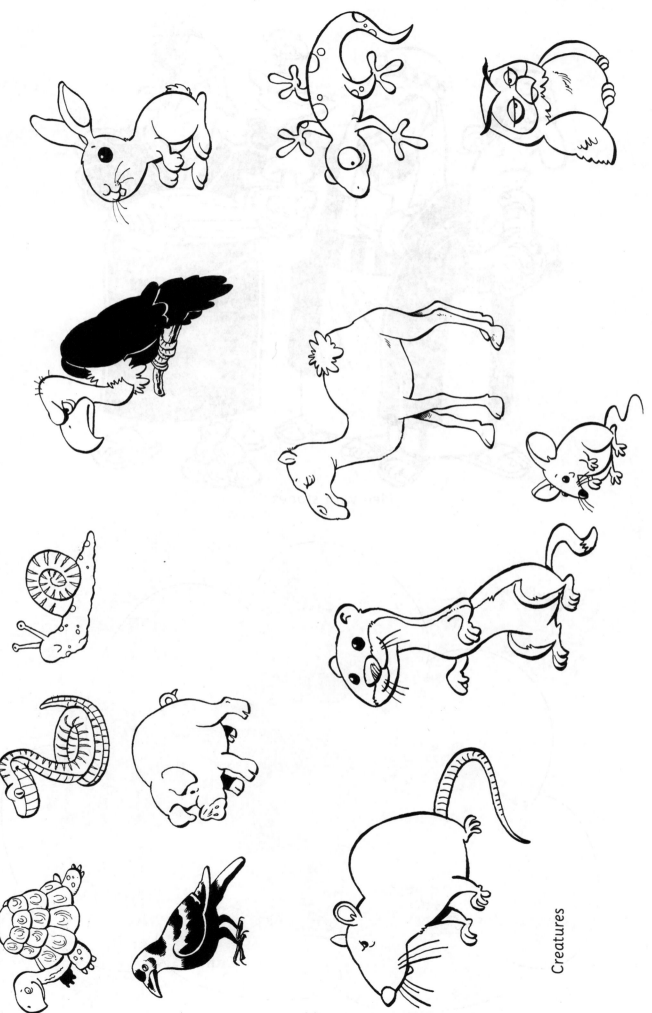

Men with stones

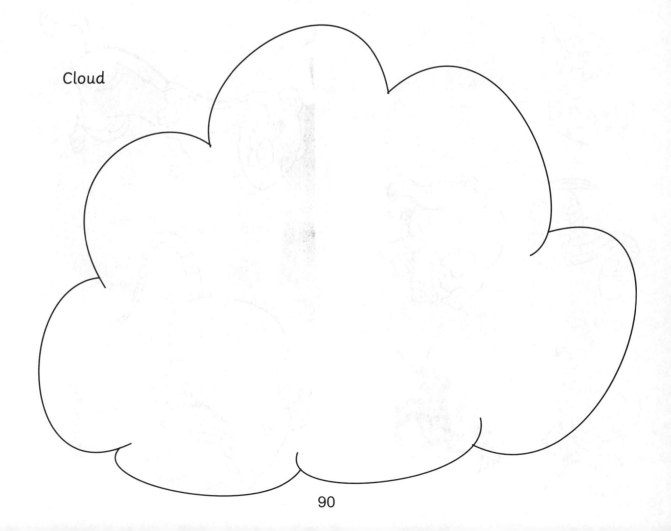

Cloud

Hill

Priests

Flame

Ethiopian Scroll

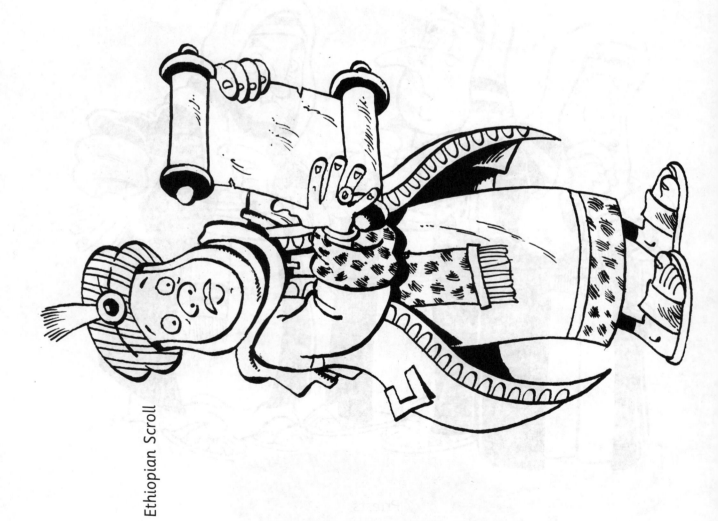

92

Saul

Peter

High Priest

93

Children's Teaching & Guidance

On The Way for 3-9s & 9-11s

We would all like our lesson plans on the Christian faith to be easier to prepare, balanced and effective. Do you also want your lessons to encourage children to view the Bible as a fascinating guide, utterly relevant to their lives? **TnT** have developed *On The Way* to be all that and more. Edited by David Jackman, *On The Way* has been used in a growing number of churches throughout the world. With the complete series, you will have all you need to give your children from age 3-9 and 9-11s a comprehensive insight to the Bible's teaching.

Benefits of *On The Way*

*   Undated material
*   Encourages leaders to study the Bible for themselves
*   Age related activities
*   Chronological approach to teaching the Bible
*   Suitable for use in Sunday Schools, Home schooling or as part of your Christian School syllabus
*   Three year syllabus

Syllabus for 3-9s

Year 1:	Book 1 (13 weeks)	In the Beginning (3); Abraham (6); Jacob (4)
	Book 2 (12 weeks)	Christmas gifts (5); Jesus' Authority (7)
	Book 3 (13 weeks)	Prayer (4); Jesus is King (5); Peter (4)
	Book 4 (10 weeks)	Joseph (4); Job (1); Moses (5)
	Book 5 (10 weeks)	In the Wilderness (4); Joshua (4); Gideon (2)
Year 2	Book 6 (10 weeks)	Samson (2); Ruth (2); Samuel (2); Saul (4)
	Book 7 (13 weeks)	The Christmas Story (4); Preparation for Service (4); The Promised Messiah (5)
	Book 8 (9 weeks)	Jesus Teaches (5); Parables of Judgment (2); The Easter Story (2)
	Book 9 (10 weeks)	David (7); Solomon (3)
	Book 10 (11 weeks)	Elijah (5); Elisha (4); Jonah (2)
Year 3	Book 11 (13 weeks)	Jesus Meets (3); God's Rules (10)
	Book 12 (14 weeks)	Heavenly Messengers (5); Jesus Helps (5); Parables of the Kingdom (4)
	Book 13 (13 weeks)	Parables of the Vineyard (3); Jesus our Redeemer (3); The Early Church (3); Paul (4)
	Book 14 (14 weeks)	Kings (5); Daniel (4); Esther (2); Nehemiah (3).

Look out for the four Games books that accompany this series! Flexible enough to be used with any syllabus.

Syllabus for 9-11s

Year 1:	Book 1 (18 weeks)	Psalms (3); In the Beginning - God (5); New Beginnings (6); Prophecy Fulfilled? (4)
	Book 2 (15 weeks)	Life in Bible Times (5); Investigating the Truth (10)
	Book 3 (20 weeks)	The Early Church (4); Paul's Fellow-workers (3); Prayer (4); Parables (7); From Here to Eternity (2)
Year 2	Book 4 (18 weeks)	Psalms (3); Samuel (3); Proverbs (3); Return to the Promised Land (5); Christmas Questions (4)
	Book 5 (21 weeks)	John the Baptist (2); Jesus is King (5); Peter (14)
	Book 6 (14 weeks)	The Holy Spirit (6); The Existence of God (1); How God should be Worshipped (5); Job and the Problem of Suffering (2).

Also available: On The Way for 11-14 year olds:

Book 1 (28 weeks); Book 2 (25 weeks); Book 3 (28 weeks); Book 4 (25 weeks); Book 5 (26 weeks); Book 6 (27 weeks).

For more information about On the Way material, please contact TnT Ministries, 34A Market House, Kingston-upon-Thames, Surrey, KY1 1JH. Tel: +44 (0) 20 8549 4967. E-mail: sales@tntministries.org.uk

or Christian Focus Publications, Geanies House, Fearn, Tain, Ross-shire, IV20 1TW. Tel: 01862 871 011 Fax: 01862 871 699. E-mail: info@christianfocus.com

Other Titles in the Series

Both these books have superb games, thoughtful activities and a thorough explanation of the gospel message. This is material that brings children to focus on fun, faith and God's forgiveness.

God's Zoo

In the amazing world of *God's Zoo* you will come across a sneaky snake, a troublesome sheep, as well as the real facts about a watery rescue mission.

There's another rescue going on called Salvation - and you'll find out about that in *God's Zoo* too. From Creation to the Cross the real story is here and it's not watered down.

ISBN: 978-1-84550-069-6

God's Secret Agent - Joseph

In the amazing world of *God's Secret Agent* you will come across kidnap and adventure, amazing secrets and some weird and wonderful dreams! (Watch out for Pharaoh's very hungry cows!)

ISBN: 978-1-84550-113-6

CF4•K
Because you're never too young to know Jesus

Christian Focus Publications publishes books for adults and children under its four main imprints: Christian Focus, Mentor, Christian Heritage and CF4K. Our books reflect that God's Word is reliable and Jesus is the way to know him, and live forever with him.

Our children's publication list includes a Sunday school curriculum that covers pre-school to early teens; puzzle and activity books. We also publish personal and family devotional titles, biographies and inspirational stories that children will love.

If you are looking for quality Bible teaching for children then we have an excellent range of Bible story and age specific theological books.

From pre-school to teenage fiction, we have it covered!

Find us at our web page: www.christianfocus.com

T n T

TnT Ministries (which stands for Teaching and Training Ministries) was launched in February 1993 by Christians from a broad variety of denominational backgrounds who are concerned that teaching the Bible to children be taken seriously. The leaders were in charge of a Sunday School of 50 teachers at St Helen's Bishopgate, an evangelical church in the City of London, for 13 years, during which time a range of Biblical teaching material has been developed. TnT Ministries also runs training days for Sunday School teachers.